I DARE YOU!

How To Stay Young Forever

Lucile Bogue

*For Nancy —
with best wishes
for sharing fun
as long as you
live! ("Fun" is
a main ingredient
for youth)
Love,
Auntie Cile
1991*

BRISTOL PUBLISHING ENTERPRISES, INC.
San Leandro, California

Printed in the United States of America.

ISBN 1-55867-017-3

Cover photography: The Imagemaker
Cover design: Frank Paredes

Acknowledgments

My heartfelt gratitude goes to many wonderful people, whose way of living inspired me to tell of them in the pages of this book: Flavia Champe, George Burns, Katsuhiko Nakajima, Beverly Sills, Ruth and Griff Greffenius, Dr. Marian Diamond, Dexter and Minu Mast, Margaret Camajani, Mabel King, Susan Thompson, Stewart Kandell, Art Anderson, Bill Cosby, Norman Cousins, Mary Elizabeth Gillespie, Norman Vincent Peale, Mary and Franklin Folsom, Cliff Wolfe, Virginia Russ, Emma Selch, Nellie Duffy, Kay Kawaguchi, Agnes de Mille, Bonnie Bogue, Caedmon Cebulski, Dora Flack, George and Marian Tolles, Sharon and Tom Young, Rev. Johanna Boeke, Eleanor Bliss, B.Jo Kinnick, Louise and Spencer Prange, Ramayeo Yeomans, Jeanne and Mike Miles, Helen Howell Parnell, Dr. Earl D. Smith, Ruby and Cecil Rorex, Genevieve German, Norma Stauffer, Lucile and Art Isitt, Felix Kuhner, Jean Brown, Winona Perry-Smith, Frances McClatchy.

Others whose work I wish to acknowledge during my ten years of research which went into the writing of this book are the following individuals and organizations whose contributions to the world of health and inspiration are herein quoted and/or referred to: Dr. Ray H. Roseman, Dr. Ralph Paffenberger, Jr., American Heart Association, American Lung Association, Arthritis Foundation, American Podiatric Medical Association, Dr. Ray J. Shephard, Dr. Charles Eichenberg, *Prevention* Magazine, *National Geographic*, Dr. Alexander Leaf, Dr. Linus Pauling, Linus Pauling Institute of Science and Medicine, Dr. Robert Giller, Wm. Morrow and Co., Gloria Swanson, William Attwood, Dr. Robert Good, Sloan-Kettering Cancer Hospital, Atheneum, Dustin Hoffman, Charles Inlander, People's Medical Society, Benita Bristol, Erma Bombeck, Dr. Joyce Brothers, *Harper's Bazaar*, Sophia Loren, Kare De Crow, Charles Schulz, Dr. Hans Selye, American Institute of Stress, Dr. Paul J. Rosch, Sangyo Noritsu University, Patrice Horn, *Psychology Today*, Strawberry Hill Press, *Bulletin of the New York Academy of Medicine*, Dr. Art Uline, Dr. Paul Lachance, Rutger's Cook College, Garson Kanin, Barbara

Cartland, Dr. Ewan Cameron, W.W. Norton, Sally Tubac, Dr. Fritz Schmerl, Leo Buscaglia, Dr. Bernie Siegel, College Avenue Players, Dr. K. Warner Schaire, Dr. Ronald Mervis, Ohio State University's Brain Aging Research Center, University of New Mexico School of Medicine, Dr. James Fries, Stanford Medical Center, Harvard School of Medicine, Elderhostel, Inc., Pennsylvania State University, University of California/Berkeley, Dr. Seuss, Carolyn North, *Regeneration Newsletter*, Helen Crackmay, *Modern Maturity*, Meir Schneider, Ph.D., Johns Hopkins University, Dr. Martin E.P. Seligman, University of Pennsylvania, Colorado Mountain College, San Jose State University, Amtrack, Wagons Ho! Wagon Train, Mrs. R. Sheldon Jones, AARP, Mississippi Queen, Aaron Copeland, Natalie Gulbrandsen, Maggi Kuhn, Carl Simonton, M.D., Cancer and Counseling and Research Center, Chaparral House, Mary Jean Froelich, Elizabeth Jodge Rees, M.D., Charlotte Orr Howard, Hemlock Society, Gov. Richard Lamm (CO), World Federation of Right-to-Die Societies, Willard Scott, National Broadcasting Co., *The Sunday Herald* (Carmel), Newell Brown, University of California/Los Angeles.

TABLE OF CONTENTS

1. GET PAID TO PLAY

This afternoon I received a gift in the mail. As I took it from the envelope, I gasped with delight. It was a beautiful book.

Innocents on Broadway, by Flavia Waters Champe, with a photograph of a dancer in a swirl of chiffon on the cover. That lovely girl was Flavia at 19, dancing with exuberance and joie de vivre. My heart soared with her.

Flavia celebrated her 88th birthday in April. *Innocents on Broadway* is the story of her first three years as a professional dancer, the beginning of a career spanning over 50 years. The book closes as she leaves the touring act to return home to marry John Champe, a young Lincoln business man.

What the book doesn't tell is that while Flavia built up a highly successful ballet school (which she operated for the next 54 years), John went on to Columbia to get a degree in anthropology and to become a professor at the University of Nebraska.

They combined their two passions, dance and anthropology, to form a new profession, the detailed

1

study of the ceremonial dances of the Indians of Northern New Mexico.

Instead of going into swift decline after John's death, as so many elderly widows do, Flavia wrote a book based on their years of happy research together, entitled *The Matachines Dance of the Upper Rio Grande: History, Music and Choreography*, brilliantly illustrated by their photos (University of Nebraska Press, 1983.)

Nothing has ever daunted this lovely lady. When she was 70, she studied ballet at the Royal Academy of Dance in London. And now in her 80s she has published two stunning books on the love of her life, dance (and has been awarded an honorary doctor's degree by the U. of N. as a result).

Love What You Do

If you're one of those lucky people who love their profession, you are on your way to staying young forever. It really doesn't make any difference what kind of work you do; if you wake up in the morning eager to get at it, you're A-OK. You may tinker with the innards of automobiles, give piano lessons, write novels, play in a jazz band, teach 10-year-olds, chisel stone, or direct shows — it doesn't matter. Just *love* it. Marcellus Merrill fell in love with automobiles when still in short pants. He remembered with delight the first car he ever saw, when a neighbor brought home the first motored vehicle in western Colorado, driving it from Denver across two mountain passes on rugged wagon trails. The man parked it in his cow barn on the hill above town, where the awe-struck natives came to gaze in wonder.

"Show us how the danged thing works," suggested one. The proud owner cranked it to start the motor, then jumped in and forged ahead, full throttle, through the back end of the barn and down over a hundred-foot embankment into the chicken yard of the startled family below. Young Marcellus was hooked on cars from that moment on.

He spent the rest of his life in an ardent love affair with autos. Today the automobile industry rolls on dozens of his patented inventions. At 75 he admitted, when asked about his latest invention, "It looks like I may have stumbled on to something." The new "something" was a "brain compartment" which, when added to the computer of the Merrill wheel aligner used in automobile assembly lines, made instant repairs if the aligner broke down. A note to Merrill from General Motors was found tucked into a large order: "You've got to keep going. If you shut down we'll be forced to."

He kept inventing well into his 80s.

Some Call Them Bums

Steamboat Springs is bursting at the seams with young people who beg to work — pump gas, or shovel snow, or wait tables, or make beds, or serve cocktails. Why do they do this work with such enthusiasm? They love it, because in their off hours they ski. That's why they are there. The natives call them "ski bums," but they are people who have learned to love what they do, so that they can do what they love. Many of them have become Olympic skiers and FIS contenders.

It's the same in New York City. The handsome young man who sells books in Scribner's is an enthusiastic salesman. Although books aren't his thing, he loves the work, because it helps him to do what he loves above all else, to dance in a small modern dance company.

The radiant waitress who brings us our chicken sandwich in the garden restaurant near Central Park seems to love her work, and we become real friends before lunch is over, even exchanging addresses. She is delighted to find I write plays, for she is an actress, arranging her work schedule in order to be available for try-outs. She loves her customers.

If you can't find work you really love, try to find a way to love the work you do.

Work Only Works if the Work You Work at Doesn't Feel Like Work

Thus spake George Burns in his wise and witty book, *Dr. Burns' Prescription for Happiness*. He illustrates this premise by describing one of the biggest challenges of his life, becoming a dramatic actor at 79 in the part of Al Lewis in *The Sunshine Boys*. He had always been a stand-up comedian.

"The hard part of movie acting is not only feeling the emotions you are to convey, but feeling them when the director yells 'Action!' Then one day it all came to me. If the director wants me to cry, I think of my sex life. If he wants me to laugh, I think of my sex life. Olivier has his system, I have mine."

In other words, George Burns gets paid for what he adores doing — making people laugh. That's why he's going strong at 92.

Music Takes the Cake (Birthday)

Ever hear the Preservation Hall Jazz Band? If you like

to stamp and clap and cheer your heart out, attend one of their concerts. This sweet-sad-exuberant music comes out of the turn-of-the-century street parades, saloons, and river boats of New Orleans, born in the hearts of people who worked and danced, laughed and cried. It's the music played by men who worked all day on the docks, and played their horns most of the night.

Preservation Hall jazz literally commands the audience to shout and leap to their feet. Not written music, it is created from the souls of the men who play it, men who made musical history in New Orleans half a century ago and are still playing. Average age, 81!

No matter how you cut it, your birthday cake will bloom with more candles each year if your work is satisfying and pleasant, if you're glad to be going back each morning. If you resent it, your health is sure to suffer, and as a consequence your work will suffer, making it more difficult each day, a vicious cycle.

It Needn't Be Music

Take Minnie Hertzog, who was born in South Dakota Territory in 1893. She began teaching when still a teenager, and never stopped, except for a short time when her two sons were small.

"No child is incapable of learning anything the teacher is capable of teaching," was her motto.

And teach them she did, generation after generation, one of the few really great teachers I have ever known. Although compulsory retirement was 65 at the time, she somehow confused the authorities by her impish "forgetfulness" concerning her age, and continued doing what she loved — opening the minds of ten-year-olds to the wonders of science and literature, to fascinating conundrums in mathematics and the English language, and, most importantly, to the honor of moral integrity. School policy didn't catch up with her until she was 76 and going strong. Lucky kids!

Minnie lived to be 95, delighting her friends with her rapier wit and incisive views on a shaky world.

Words Can Do It

Adela Rogers St. John, the journalist and flamboyant writer who covered the Patty Hearst abduction story at 87, began her career as a newspaper reporter when she was 13 years old.

"Anyone can live as long as he wants," asserted the feisty octagenarian, who at an earlier age almost destroyed herself with drink. Then she joined Alcoholics Anonymous and lived to write again with fervor. "It's all up to you."

"But how do you stay so youthful?"

"Work!" she responded. "And love your work! No reason for despair. There are always so many wonderful surprises ahead!"

Square Peg

If you're a square peg in a round hole, with your corners wearing thin from the rub, it's never too late to change.

A handsome young friend in Tokyo confided to me that he hated his job selling stocks for a large brokerage firm. His parents were very proud of their son's career. He was set in the path of success. And in Japan, once one has set his foot upon a certain path,

6

starting in kindergarden, leading to the "right" elementary school, leading to the "right" high school, leading to the "right" university and eventually the "right" job, there is no deviation. But I didn't know that.

I asked Katsuhiko why he hated his job.

"I have to be dishonest," he admitted. "I have to tell my clients things that aren't true. I hate myself."

"Why not change?" I asked. "You're only twenty-two. Young enough to change careers."

He stared at me in shocked disbelief.

"But we *never* change jobs! People don't do that!"

"In America we do. There's no point in spending your life at something you hate."

He shook his head, not quite believing what he had heard. Job hopping isn't part of the Japanese culture. But I couldn't bear to watch this beautiful young man turned into an embittered and weary old man by work he hated. I continued subtly to encourage him to find some escape. At last we hit upon a plan. He would go back to the university to get a master's degree, and in the process, make a career change. His family and friends couldn't fault him for that.

Today he works for a big oil importing firm, in charge of dispatching oil tankers all over the globe in quest of Japan's precious oil supply. An exciting job, with new and unexpected challenges facing him each day.

Work You Hate Can Make You Sick

Being forced to work every day at a job you despise builds up emotional stress that triggers the "fight or flight" syndrome, setting off a series of chemical reactions in the body which, if bottled up without "fighting" or "fleeing," can seriously injure or even destroy the human mechanism. Some results of this destructive stress which *Prevention Magazine* reported in just one year (1985) included angina, arrhythmia (irregular heart beat, sometimes fatal), high cholesterol levels, fibrositis (stepchild of rheumatic disease), irritable bowel syndrome, excessive sweating, wrinkles, lowered immunity to disease, and migraine headaches. Add to that list arthritis, as well as other undiagnosed aches and pains that carve suffering lines in the face, a slump to the back, and the general feeling and appearance of old age. Better do something about an unhappy job while you're still ahead.

Is it any wonder then that avoiding all that will actually keep you younger longer?

Take Piute Pete. Peter Kaufman was a sickly young fellow in his early twenties, trying desperately to hold down an office job in New York. Each day was an ordeal, for he suffered acutely with arthritis. Finally his doctor recommended he join a square dance club. One night, when the caller didn't show up, Pete took over at the mike. That was the beginning of a 50-year career as Piute Pete, the famous square dance caller. He quit his dull job in the office, and his arthritis miraculously diappeared.

"It just goes to show," he grinned, "how anyone can change misfortune like my arthritis and that dull job, into something happy and good, if you do a little striving in the right direction."

The Man that I Married

Art was a teacher when we were married. As a third-generation teacher, I presumed that all teachers loved their profession. It wasn't until after we were married that he confessed how intensely he hated it. He didn't understand children; he disliked and distrusted them. The feeling was mutual. And his stomach ulcer was killing him.

By sheer accident, he fell into a position at mid-life, after years of groping around for a change, as manager of the Northwest Colorado branch of the Federal Land Bank. It was a job that fitted him like his skin, driving over the vast expanse of northwestern Colorado, talking with farmers, getting to know them and their problems and ambitions, and returning to the office to work with maps and mathematical reports. That took care of the ulcer.

Love Your Work

Whether you're a cattle rancher in Wyoming or a surgical nurse in San Francisco, a secretary in Alaska or a car salesman in Alabama, if you love what you're doing, you're on your way to staying young as long as you live. Love it or leave it.

Bill Lear, designer of the Lear jet, was at his drawing board designing plans for the new economy prop jet when he said, "Love what you're doing and do what you love. Measure success not by how much money you're making, but by how much fun you're having."

Bill Lear was 75.

Extra Tips:

The Right Job, Robert Snelling, Viking, NY, 1987. A career
     counselor advises you to work at a job you love,
     and tells you how to find it.

> *We ought to dance with rapture*
> *that we should be alive.*
> —D.H. Lawrence

2. Let's Tango

We were having tea in Helen Parnell's elegant flat in Antibes, with the sweet scent of mimosa drifting in through the open French doors. Late afternoon sun glittered on the Bay of Angels, and the rosy city of Nice shone across the bay.

I had been staying with Helen a few days, doing an interview for a book in which she was to appear, *Dancers on Horseback*.

Virginia Gallico, another guest, widow of the late Paul Gallico (author of *Snow Goose* and *Mrs. 'arris Goes to Paris*), sipped her tea and looked lovely, although a bit tired. She had just come back from a busy day at the Palace in Monaco, where she had long been Princess Grace's lady-in-waiting and confidante, and now that Grace was gone, she continued on, helping Prince Rainier keep the household on an even keel.

Helen, tiny and chic in a fashionable hostess gown, clicked back and forth to the kitchen on four-inch spike heels, replenishing the supply of hors d'oeuvres and tea. The other guests were a charming young British couple on a holiday, whose parents had worshipped Helen Howell Parnell during her heyday as the reigning dancer at the Palladium in London.

I had been poring over Helen's scrapbooks, newspaper accounts of her triumphs throughout Europe, her command performance before King George V and Queen Mary, her story-book marriage to

Valentine Parnell, wealthy theater magnate and director of the Palladium, and her dazzling life in the circles of London's high society.

Here was pretty heady company. I felt as though I were watching a movie. It wasn't real.

"Helen, do you still tango?" ventured the young man shyly.

Without a word, Helen walked over to the fireplace. With a graceful flip of her long skirt, she tossed a luscious leg high in the air, and rested her heel on the mantelpiece above her head. We all gasped.

"No, I don't tango any more," she laughed over her shoulder. "But I do my exercises and I play golf every day."

Helen was 80 years old.

The Joys of Dance

Anyone who enjoyed the dazzling pyrotechnics of the South American dance company *Tango Argentino*, which fired their North American audiences recently with amazing tango routines, knows what prowess went into their show. But even more mind-boggling than the beauty of the dance was the fact that the dancers were all "middle-aged" people.

The late Walter Terry, dance critic for *Saturday Review*, recounted an interview he had with Ruth St. Dennis, who, with her contemporary, Isadora Duncan, changed the dance world forever. She was still performing at 90, just a few weeks before her death.

"I don't expect to live forever," she told him, "although all present signs point to the contrary." She had just completed a stretch split, which most of us would find impossible at any age.

Why Do Dancers Stay Young?

Then there's Shirley McLaine. At 50, an age when my grandmother was a gray, weary old lady dressed in black mourning, Shirley danced up a storm across country in a one-woman show. For the entire evening she was never off stage, but sang, pattered, danced and chattered for two hours, a grueling stint for a 16-year-old. Her gorgeous legs and exuberance had the audiences walking out of the theaters feeling 20 years younger.

How do dancers do it? By *using* every day these wonderful bodies with which we are gifted. The old cliché is true, "Use it, or lose it!" Exercise! Exercise! Exercise!

Today I talked with Jeanne Fuller Miles, who danced on the Orpheum Circuit in the '20s with Helen Parnell and Flavia Waters. A trim attractive blonde, with a clean smooth skin and sparkling eyes, she is active in Hill Barn Theater, which she helped found decades ago. When she mentioned that she was past 80, I almost fell off the phone. I could have figured it out for myself, but I found it hard to believe. And husband Mike, as lively and spirited at Jeanne, is 89.

"How do you do it?" I asked when I called her back to see if I had heard correctly.

"We play golf every day. I was out yesterday, even though it was sprinkling. And Mike is out today."

Amazing Alicia Alonzo is today the brightest star in Cuba. Where the Cuban people used to have pictures of the Holy Madonna tacked to their walls, now it is dance posters of the popular ballerina, Alicia. Although 69 and almost totally blind, she is still the *prima ballerine assoluta*, dancing with the fire and passion that captivated audiences and critics when she danced with the American Ballet Theater, as well as in Broadway musicals 40 years ago in New York. She celebrated her 60th birthday by performing the full-length Giselle, with all the leaps and pirouettes.

"I plan to be 200," she says. There seems to be no reason to doubt her.

But I Don't Dance

Okay. Neither did Paul Gallico. A writer's life is of necessity a sedentary one. And if the writer is as prolific as Gallico, that means hours on end, literally. But he was as athletic as his career allowed. In his early days, when he was a sports columnist for *The New York Daily News*, he staged a bout for himself with Jack Dempsey (who knocked him out in one minute and 37 seconds), a swimming race with Johnny Weismuller, and a golf match with Bobby Jones. But his favorite sport was fencing, in which he was a champion.

"On my 75th birthday," he wrote, "I won two out of three fencing matches from a professional in London. One of these, I suspect, was a birthday gift, but the final one, which I took 5-3, was for blood."

Shortly before his death, he wrote the best-selling novel and movie hit, *The Poseidon Adventure*, active and alert and productive to the end of his long life. How was he able to stay youthful and full of writing enthusiasm? He kept *moving*.

Writer's Secret

I live in a nine-room house, built on a steep California hillside, on five different levels. Everywhere I go, I must go up or down a flight of stairs, which keeps me flexible. I also take an hour's walk each day up and down the steep street to the shops and mail box. I can usually think up a good excuse for *having* to take that long hard climb. And after I get started, I love it — the neighbors' flowers, the towers of San Francisco rising out of the mists, the softly etched beauty of Golden Gate Bridge. That walk, along with the rest of my regime, has enabled me to lose more than 30 pounds during the past three years without dieting.

I used to think, "I don't have *time* to exercise! I'm much too busy." But now I don't have time *not* to. Exercising takes less time than trips to the doctor, and it's much more fun and less expensive.

Extra Years of Youth

Harvard School of Medicine has made an amazing discovery. In a study of 17,000 of their alumni, they have found that those who work out regularly have half the risk of death as those who do little or no exercise. Energetic activity three or four times a week reduces high blood pressure, inherited tendency toward early death, or even the negative effects of cigarette smoking to some extent, Harvard reports in *The New England Journal of Medicine*.

Those who walk five to ten miles a week cut down their death risk 10%, while those who walk 30 to 35 miles or more cut down their death rate over 50%, claims Harvard.

Although the world offers a marvelous smorgasbord of ways to exercise, walking seems to be the best all-round answer. In the first place it takes no skill or specialized training. It doesn't require an expensive gymnasium or locker rent. It has no geographic or climatic requirements. It doesn't call for a special wardrobe. All you need is a pair of sneakers and the gumption to get out and *do it*. Time is the only prerequisite. The time is all yours, and so is the decision about how you use it, whether to spend an hour or so a day now, enjoying a good brisk walk, or to spend your later years in a walker, wheel chair or hospital bed.

Walk for Your Life

Ten years ago the watchword of the '70s was "run for your life." James A. Fixx's book, *Complete Book of Running*, was America's fitness bible. Everyone seemed to be into running: mothers and grandmothers, marathon champions and airline pilots, invalids and waiters.

Every morning before he went to work as a waiter at the posh St. Frances Hotel in San Francisco, Larry Lewis would run six miles through Golden Gate Park. And he was 100.

Eula Weaver at 81 was an invalid with heart trouble. Hooked by Fixx, she began running, and seven years later she captured Senior Olympics gold medals for the mile and half mile. Fixx was everyone's guru. American had invented a new religion. His followers could be seen on every highway and byway, their mouths agape, their faces tortured and twisted, their arms and legs flailing, the sweat flying.

But that was before death-by-jogging hit the headlines. There were 59-year-old Congressman Goodloe Byron of Maryland, 58-year-old Carl H. Madden (former chief economist for the U.S. Chamber of Commerce), and 43-year-old aerospace engineer, Keith P. Kerney, all in the Washington, D.C. area. But the cruelest blow of all was when Fixx himself succumbed.

Now doctors are warning people, especially older runners, to cool it. Dr. Ray H. Roseman, a San Francisco cardiologist, calls jogging "a miserable post-collegiate athletic travesty that has already killed scores, possibly hundreds." Less spectacular but even more prevalent are the frequent injuries to joints, especially those in the feet, knees, hips and back. There are also serious sprains and pulled tendons. Perhaps the most serious is the shin splint, or stress fracture, in which the leg actually breaks itself, caused by the violent pulling of the calf muscle on the shin bone. This occurs not only with older runners, but with collegiate athletes as well.

Dr. Ralph Paffenberger Jr. of Stanford's School of Medicine told the American Heart Association that if individuals burn up 2,000 calories a week, they can reduce the risk of heart attack by 64%. But you needn't run to do it. The same thing can be accomplished by five hours of bicycling or five hours of walking. No need to kill yourself to stay young!

"Three miles of brisk walking will accomplish the same thing as three miles of jogging," says C. Carson Conrad, executive director of the President's Council on Physical Fitness.

Gentler Trails

Now, instead of telling heart patients to "take it easy," doctors urge them to start a regular brisk walking regime. Such organizations as the American Heart Association, American Lung Association, Arthritis Foundation, American Podiatric Medical Association, and the President's Council on Physical Fitness and Sports are broadcasting the word: "Walk and get well!"

Happily seniors are at the forefront of this wave of fitness.

How About the Malls?

In some cities, authorities have inaugurated the perfect solution for those who don't walk because of icy streets or fear of muggers, a very real threat in many metropolitan areas. It is the "mall walk," for which shopping malls open early in the morning, before the stores open and the shoppers arrive. Here the weather is never inclement and the security system is patrolled. Who could ask for anything more?

"We don't have to worry about dogs, traffic, rocks, hills or pollen," beams Helen Gulledge, 69, who suffers with arthritis. Her husband, Luther, 75, who has heart trouble, accompanies her for a brisk two-mile walk every morning in the Haywood Mall in Greenville, S.C.

Often mall walkers organize in groups. One such is the Go Getters, a spirited bunch that patrols the Galleria in Glendale, California, just after daybreak. They don't even turn to view the window displays, for that only slows them down. One laughs, "I could have walked to San Francisco by now." Don't get in their way or they might run you down.

Turn Back the Clock 25 Years

The New York Times carried a story in 1986 quoting authorities who claimed that the middle-aged and elderly can literally turn back the age clock 10 to 25 years just by walking. "Half an hour's brisk walk three or four times a week can provide ten years of rejuvenation," says Dr. Roy J. Shephard, expert on exercising and aging at the University of Toronto. Walking lowers the resting heart rate, increases the amount of blood pumped through the heart, and places stress on the bones, which raises the calcium content, thus decreasing the danger of fracture, one of the most foreboding threats of old age.

I am living proof of the last claim. I have fallen downstairs and knocked myself out; I fell on a cruise ship and dislocated my shoulder; I took a stunning fall on a bird-watching hike in Arizona; and I have had four severe falls on city pavement. (I move too fast for my trifocals.) But the only broken bone I sustained was my nose. Not bad at the age when many end up flat on their backs in hospital beds with broken hips!

Why Not Join the Club?

Dr. Charles Eichenberg, of the New Start Health Center in St. Petersburg, Florida, read of the Walking Club in *Prevention*. Convinced that walking is a prescription for just about everything, including high blood pressure, high cholesterol, diabetes, weight loss, stabilizing blood sugar at lower levels, balancing blood fats, and improving a long list of intestinal ills — colitis, diverticulitis, gastritis, and spastic colon — Dr. Eichenberg now has New Start give every member a complimentary membership to Prevention Walking Club. for only $10.95 you too can join the thousands walking back to youth. Address: Prevention Walking Club, 33 E. Minor St., Emmaus, PA 18098. You'll receive your *Walking Club Magazine*, newsletters and other goodies to keep you going.

Whatever You Do, Enjoy It!

There are countless ways of keeping the old bod polished up and running smoothly. The key word is "enjoy." If you don't enjoy it, if you look on that daily exercise as a disagreeable job that must be done, you'll soon become bored. And if you're bored, forget it. You will anyway.

Choose something you *love* doing! Get a horse! Eleanor Bliss, 90, saddles up and rides out along the mountain trails daily, except when the snow gets too deep around Sky-High Ranch, her home 7,000 feet up in the Colorado Rockies. She comes home radiant and smiling, her cheeks rosy from the brisk air.

One of the loveliest sights I ever witnessed was a group of seniors skimming over the ice at the skating rink one winter afternoon at Rockefeller Plaza, their bodies swaying in graceful rhythm to a Vienna waltz. They were as trim and finely tuned as their younger companions, and appeared to be enjoying themselves even more.

Gertrude Fetcher can be found every weekend in the nine-month winter on her cross-country skis, not on Steamboat's famous ski slopes, but swinging out across hill and valley through silent mountain snow, her face alight and her hair shining silver in the sun. If you can walk, you can cross-country ski without expensive alpine skis, special clothing, or lift tickets. And it's fun!

Some People Love Tennis

In the early 1970's, Super-Seniors was organized, a group for tennis nuts 60 and over, and then 70, and now 80. At that point Super-Senior President C. Alphonso Smith ("Smitty") took two of his hot flashes, Henry Doyle, 81, and Travis Smith, 80, to England to challenge a team of British octogenarians, as a side event to the Wimbledon Tournament.

You needn't be a young flawless athlete to play tennis. Charles Chaffee, 75, plays while wearing a steel-ribbed corset to support a displaced vertebra. Travis Smith had to have his pacemaker replaced by a more powerful model to keep up with him on the court. Buddy Goeltz, 71, has a hearing aid which doesn't pick up the linesman's calls, but he can still defeat Sam Shore, also 71. Bitsy Grant, 66, who was a member of the U.S. Davis Cup team in the '30s, has had cataract operations on both eyes and must wear dark glasses and a visor on the court.

Or Would You Rather Be a Fish?

Dorothy Wither was up at 5:30 every morning, winter and summer, to drive a mile to the indoor swimming pool, where she swam for a vigorous hour before getting dressed to go to work in her swanky dress shop. She and George Tolles had personal keys to the pool and year round, regardless of weather or sub-zero temperatures, they took the plunge. No one has kept track of how many years Dorothy maintained this rigorous routine, but she swam up to the day of her death at age 84, as youthful and beautiful as ever.

I celebrated my 70th birthday by learning to snorkle in the crystal green waters of Tahiti. I'd always wanted to be a fish, and there I became one, moving easily through coral forests and swaying seaweed. My companions were the fish, arrayed in their dazzling variety of brilliant colors. It was so unbelievably beautiful, I almost believed I had died and gone to paradise. There's nothing like it.

Extra Tips:

Prevention Walking Club, 33 E. Minor St., Emmaus, PA 18098

Resources for Older Sports Enthusiasts (quoted by permission from AARP News Bulletin)

70+ Ski Club, Lloyd Lambert, 104 East Side Drive, Ballston Lake, NY 12019 (518) 399-5458

National Bowling Council, Lance Elliott, 1919 Pennsylvania Ave. N.W., Washington, DC 22006 (202) 659-9070

National Golf Foundation, David Huber, 1150 South U.S. Highway 1, Jupiter, FL 33408 (305) 744-6006

U.S. Senior Athletic Games, Manya Joyce, 200 Castlewood Drive, North Palm Beach, FL 33408 (314) 842-3030

U.S. Senior Olympics, 321 West Port Plaza Drive, Suite 202, St. Louis, MO (314) 576-1987

National Association of Senior Citizen Softball, Ken Maas, 40700 Romeo Plank Road, Clinton Township, MI 48044 (313) 286-8757

National Senior Sports Association, Lloyd Wright, NSSA, 117 Cameron Street, Alexandria, VA 22314 (703) 549-6711

It's the genes that determine to a great extent how long you will live. It is correct nutrition that makes the life worth living.
M.C., Allentown, PA, 70
(*People's Medical Society Health Bulletin*)

3. EAT TO STAY YOUNG AND SEXY

I flew to Ecuador to do research for a book I was writing. To support my addiction to research and writing, I taught English in the Colegio Americano in Guayaquil for a year.

But even more exciting than the *Gambling Lady* mystery I was writing was the mystery of Vilcabamba, the tiny isolated village high in the Andes. I had just read the amazing account of Dr. Alexander Leaf in *National Geographic* (January 1973), entitled "Search for the Oldest People." I was determined to see for myself. I couldn't believe it.

Vilcabamba's Mystery

Alexander Leaf, M.D., claimed that people in that remote mountain community frequently lived to be well past 100. Out of the population of 819, nine of them were over 100. That would be 1,100 centenarians for every 100,000 people, while in the United States, the figure is three for every 100,000. Dr. Leaf was Chief of Medical Services at Massachusetts General Hospital and professor at Harvard Medical School. Here was something worth looking into.

To reach Vilcabamba was not easy. First I took a small plane to Quito, threading its way through narrow canyons of the Andes. There I changed to a tiny mosquito plane for the hop to Loja, where I transferred to a Jeep, which bounced us over an almost impassable road across more mountains. Dusty and a bit bruised, we arrived in Vilcabamba.

After checking in at a primitive *posada*, I asked my guide to take me to the home of Miguel Carpio, who was 123, according to Dr. Leaf and the church's baptismal records. We found him sitting in the patio of his granddaughter's home, surrounded by a casual assortment of children, chickens, a couple of young pigs and a kid goat.

Señor Carpio grinned with pleasure as I introduced myself and squeezed his hand. I could see that he was blind, his eyes milky with cataracts, but otherwise he seemed as hale and hearty as a man of 70. Delighted to have company, he answered my questions with wit and good nature. Through my interpreter, he told me that he had served in the war against Spain to help Peru gets its freedom.

"I ran away to join the army," he chuckled, "looking for adventure. Got more that I bargained for!"

He pulled up his shirt to display a deep twisting scar that distorted his belly. His gray-haired granddaughter lighted a cigarette and handed it to him.

"Got that in Callao," he laughed again, patting his ancient wound. "A Spanish shell tore straight through my guts. They thought I was dead for sure."

"What keeps you so young?" I asked.

The kid bleated. Sr. Carpio chortled with a twinkle in his sightless eyes.

"Laughter. Wine. And loving the ladies. Of course I

can't see them any more. But I can sure feel them!" He turned suddenly serious. "But soon I'll be able to see again. The *medico norteamericano* is coming to take me to the hospital in Quito for an operation. He says I'll see like a young man."

On the way back to the *posada,* we stopped to pass the time of day with Macaela, an ancient little lady spinning a heap of snowy wool in the dooryard of her adobe house.

"*Buenas tardes, madre mia,*" my guide greeted her.

"*Buenos,*" she continued to spin busily. Her smile was shy. "But I'm not a mother. I've never been married."

"How old are you?" I asked. "People in Vilcabamba live to be very old, don't they?"

"I'm only 102," she apologized, "but I had twelve brothers who lived past 90, and my sister died at 107."

Farther along we stopped to watch Hermelinda Leon scooping hot fragrant loaves from the outdoor oven with a long wooden shovel. Only 95, she worked as hard as anyone in town, baking bread for her neighbors from dawn to dark, as well as keeping house for her niece, with whom she lived.

It was nearly sundown as we started up the hill to the *posada.* We stopped to speak to an *anciano* riding astride a load of sugar cane strapped to the back of a donkey. He carried a heavy wicked-looking machete with which he had been chopping cane since dawn.

"*Buenos tardes, padre!*" called out my guide. "How many years have you?"

"Not many," the old man laughed. "I'm one of the young ones. Only 97 years," and he rode on to deliver his cane to the sugar wheel.

Vilcabamba's Secrets

What did it mean? How did this segregated little pocket of humanity manage to out-live the rest of us? After a weekend of living in this lofty mountain valley with the villagers, I began to draw my own conclusions, unscientific as they may be.

1. They keep physically active, day in and day out. No time to grow old.
2. This activity, in that rarified mountain air, develops strong lungs and hearts, legs and backs. And excellent circulation.
3. Despite their labor, they lead a serene and tranquil existence, far from tension, pressures, pollutions and maddening noises of the modern world.
4. The elderly are loved and looked up to, their advice valued. They are a vital part of the family structure, helping with housework, cooking, baby-care, gardening and looking after the animals. They feel needed.
5. They eat sparingly, a diet low in calories, protein and fat. (Dr. Jean Mayer, Professor of Nutrition at Harvard, notes that almost all their protein and fats come from vegetable sources, rather than animal.)
6. Average daily diet of the elderly is 1,200 calories, compared to 3,300 calories for the average American. (Dr. Guillermo Vela of Quito finds they eat only 35 to 38 grams of protein, 12 to 19 grams of fat, and 200 to 260 grams of carbohydrates.)
7. They use almost no salt nor sugar.

8. There are no obese citizens in Vilcabama. Neither are there any undernourished.

9. They drink wine in moderate quantities on festive occasions; otherwise their basic drinks are herb tea, lemonade and water. Especially water. It's the water, they claim, that is their magic. "It's the iron in it that keeps us young!" they boast. "Look at these lemons. See what the water does for them!" They are almost as large as footballs.

10. But perhaps the most important element of all, they eat "living" food, without chemicals or processing. Nothing artificial.

Living Food

Has it ever occurred to you that the food you are eating may be alive? Or that the spark of life, that vital element is being transmitted to you in the form of healthful abundant vigor?

Prove it to yourself. Cut the top off a carrot and put it, top up, in a shallow dish of water in a sunny window. Soon you will have a dish of bright feathery greenery. That carrot is alive.

Cut a chunk off a raw potato and stick it in the ground somewhere. Water it, and before long you will have a healthy potato vine, capable of producing its own crop of potatoes there in the dark earth (if the temperature doesn't drop below freezing. Freezing is sure death to a plant. Does that tell you anything about frozen foods?).

I was first intrigued by this idea of "living" food when I read of grain, discovered in the ancient Egyptian tombs, coming to life and growing in the proper environment. After centuries, it still lived.

Today many nutritionists are telling us that live food is far more nutritious that processed food. The most healthful food of all is raw. Next comes food that is cooked as briefly as possible. (This means only plant foods, of course, for animal food should be thoroughly cooked to destroy harmful organisms.)

Throw Away the Sugar Bowl

I threw mine away over 40 years ago when our three-year-old daughter began to be overweight. We were fortunate to have a wise pediatrician who said, "No more dessert! No one needs them. Sugar should never have been invented!"

About the same time our dentist visited the public school where I was teaching, and gave a dental health talk.

"Never drink sweet, carbonated drinks! They're as bad for the teeth as candy! Of course, if you enjoy a toothache, and like having your teeth filled and pulled, don't bother with my advice. Eat up! Drink up! And enjoy your false teeth when you get them."

So our children grew up in a sugarless home, with the exception of holidays desserts and birthday cakes. I felt that these special occasions could do little harm.

Sugar is Poison

That's what I tell the startled Girl Scouts who come to my door, selling candy and cookies. "I'll give you a donation to help the Scouts, but not a penny for sugar."

Not only is sugar responsible for dental problems,

but it is the culprit in numerous other maladies that torment the modern American. Obesity plagues more of us that any other one problem. Fad diets are a booming business, "spas" and make-over salons a growing industry, and books on "How to Lose Weight" are perennial best-sellers. Linus Pauling, the two-time Nobel winner, says in his book, *How to Live Longer and Feel Better*, that obesity is not only an inconvenience. It more that doubles the incidence of illness, and decreases life expectancy by 10 years. What could you do with an extra 10 years?

Cholesterol is proven to be highly responsive to sugar, Pauling points out in describing a strictly scientific experiment varying the amount of sucrose (sugar) in the diets of 18 normal men. The ordinary American eats an average 100 pounds of sugar annually. Cut that down and you will improve your general good health, decrease your chances of heart disease, lower your blood cholesterol, and strenghthen your body's natural defense mechanism against all disease.

Coronary disease, including angina pectoris, says Pauling, is a disease of modern times. It has been recorded in medical literature only with the past 100 years. "The increasing incidence...closely parallels the increasing consumption of sugar."

Killer Number Six

In addition to heart disease, sugar has been proven to be conducive to the development of diabetes, the nation's No. 6 killer. Diabetes "runs in families" and is often genetically originated. However, a perfectly normal person, with no sign of diabetes in the family line, can develop diabetes by the over-use of sugar, which over-stimulates and "wears out" the pancreas, the organ that produces the insulin necessary to keep the blood sugar in balance.

Osteoporosis

This disease, so widely prevalent among the elderly, can be life-endangering as well as disfiguring. Thousands of older citizens, especially women, are admitted to emergency wards each year as a result of broken hips, arms, shoulders and backs, due to the weakening of bones, causing them to be thin and brittle. Thus a fall, or often just a quick change of position, causes a tragic break.

Sugar decreases the amount of phosphorus in the blood to such an extent that the body is unable to sustain calcification. The bones deteriorate. Women become "little old ladies" as the calcium is leached from the skeleton and the body frame shrinks. Many of these emergency room cases end in an early grave. Is your sweet tooth worth it?

The Million Dollar Book

The most valuable book in my extensive health library is Dr. Robert M. Giller's *The Medical Makeover: The Revolutionary No-Willpower Program for Lifetime Health*. A gift from my enthusiastic daughter and son-in-law, who had lost 25 pounds and 35 pounds respectively on Giller's regime, I read it with great interest. It corroberated all my own health practices. I eat almost no sugar, salt, fat, red meat, nor processed food. I had already stopped drinking alcohol two or three years earlier when I discovered that it causes the foot and leg cramps that had me leaping out of bed several times during the night. Coffee, I found, did the same thing. But I had to have my coffee! How else could I be alert and rarin' to go the first thing in the morning?

After reading Dr. Giller's *Medical Makeover*, I decided to give his plan a try.

Caffeine, the Respectable Drug

Do you have any of these symptoms that the good doctor lists as indicative of caffeine addition? Insomnia, depression, irritability, chronic fatigue, restlessness, rapid pulse or heartbeat, stomach pains or heartburn, headaches, diarrhea, anxiety? Sources of this drug are more prevalent than you might think. In addition to coffee, tea, chocolate, and colas, it is found in innumerable drugs prescribed for weight loss and pain relief, as well as in diuretics, "wake-up" tablets, and cold and allergy remedies. If you are the average American, with a hotly denied caffeine addiction, you are probably taking in 1000 milligrams or more daily. As a result, you are a prime candidate for heart disease, breast cysts, cancer, ulcers, or even mental illness.

I decided it was worth kicking the habit. Dr. Giller gently leads you through your *Medical Makeover*, week by week. I'd already given up my other "bad habits," just because I felt so marvelously good afterward. But caffeine? I was no addict!

Ha! Fortunately Dr. Giller advises you to start this some weekend when you have no commitments. Good advice! I had withdrawal symptoms like you wouldn't believe. Kicking caffeine addiction is a painful as breaking any other drug addiction. I ached. I was dizzy. I was sick for three days with "the flu." Sharon chuckled when I called her in Arizona.

"Don't worry," she laughed. "It's not flu. It's withdrawal symptoms. Everybody suffers the same way. But it's worth it. You'll see."

She was right. I felt wonderful the following week.

Just Say Yes

If you can honestly answer yes to Dr. Giller's questions, you are now already well-nourished:

1. Do you eat regular meals at regular times?
2. Do you eat breakfast?
3. Do you eat fresh fruits and vegetables daily?
4. Do you eat whole grains and fibers daily?
5. Do you read food package labels to minimize your intake of fats, sugars, and preservatives?
6. Do you avoid white-flour products?
7. Do you avoid fried foods, including fast foods?
8. Do you avoid fats such as butter, margarine, cheese, mayonnaise, oils, etc?
9. Do you eat fewer than three eggs per week?
10. Do you avoid red meats?
11. Do you avoid using table salt?

If you can't say yes to at least eight of these questions, you're in for daily fatigue, and possible heart disease and cancer. You're also lowering your natural resistance to a wide spectrum of other diseases.

Public Enemy No. 3

Can you believe it? Salt. Salt of the earth. A cherished commodity since biblical times and before. Yet is is a proven enemy of the people, raising their blood pressure to the point of strokes and heart attacks.

We all need some salt. And it does improve the taste of food. But we get far too much without realizing it. A teaspoon of salt contains 2,000 milligrams of sodium, a safe amount for one day. Yet Dr. Giller estimates that most of us get up to 6,900 milligrams daily. It is found in monosodium glutamate (*Accent*), antacids, baking soda, practically all prepared and canned foods, cereals, bakery goods, frozen dinners, bread, crackers and fast foods.

Chemistry: Friend or Enemy?

When I was a junior in high school, I won a national essay contest with a paper entitled, "Chemistry in the Relation to the Enrichment of Life." I was naive and thrilled by the wonders of the future in the field of chemistry. But I didn't know the widespread harm that arises out of that same magician's bottle of chemicals. Most people still don't realize what is happening to them as a result.

Chemicals, in the form of preservatives, artificial coloring and artificial flavoring, are implicated in many diseases — arthritis, migraine headache, colitis, cancer, mental problems, and hyperactivity.

As Gloria Swanson says, "I want nothing that's been sprayed, dyed, gassed or preserved with wax! I don't want it. My body doesn't want it. Just because something's on a plate doesn't mean it's good for you!"

Gloria Swanson, silent-screen movie star of the '20s, is still glamorous at 88. Long a nutrition advocate, she is as outspoken about her food as she is about her many love affairs and her six husbands.

What About Sex?

Yes, I know I promised that eating right would help you stay young and sexy. Okay. If you're youthful, healthy, and bursting with enthusiasm, you are sexy! Malnourished droopy people, obsessed with their ill health, are certainly not very attractive to either sex.

Youthful Gloria Swanson married her sixth husband at the age of 79. It's never too late. She credits her continuing beauty and feminine appeal to her concern with proper nutrition.

"You can stay young and sexy if you eat right. Or you can destroy yourself with bad food habits."

Extra Reading on Foods:

Dr. Atkins' Diet Revolution, Robert C. Atkins, M.D., Bantam Books, NY 1973

The Eater's Digest: The Consumer's Factbook of Food Additives, Michael F. Jacobson, Manchor Books/ Doubleday, Garden City, NY 1972

Eat Well, Get Well, Stay Well, Carlton Frederick, Ph.D., Grosset and Dunlap, NY, 1980

Human Life Styling: Keeping Whole in the 20th Century, John C. McCamy, M.D., and James Presley, Harper and Row, 1975

Introduction to Clinical Allergy, Ben F. Feingold, M.D., Thomas, Springfield, IL, 1973

Know Your Nutrition, Linda Clark, Keats Pub. Co. Inc., New Canaan, CT, 1973

Let's Eat Right to Keep Fit, Adelle Davis, Harcourt Brace and World, 1954. Practical guide to nutrition for good health through diet.

Let's Get Well, Adelle Davis, Harcourt Brace and World, 1965. Renewing health through nutrition, by the foremost pioneer in the field.

The Medical Makeover: The Revolutionary No-Willpower

Program for Lifetime Health, Robert M. Giller, M.D., (Beechtree Books), William Morrow and Co., NY, 1986. Truly a "million dollar book," a zinger. Best advice you'll ever get.

Nutrition Action Newsletter, Center for Science in the Public Interest, 1501 16th St. NW, Washington, DC 20036 ($15 annual subscription)

The Pulse Test, Arthur F. Coca, M.D., Lyle Stuart Inc., Secaucus, NJ, 1982. The secret of building your basic health by eliminating your allergic foods, thus eliminating hives, high blood pressure, diabetes, ulcers, epileptic seizures, migraine headache, dizziness, backache, constipation, depression, and "that tired feeling."

Spirulina, The Whole Food Revolution, Larry Switzer, Bantam Books, 1982. Remarkable food from the sea; may help solve problems of world hunger and poor health.

Why Your Child Is Hyperactive, Ben F. Feingold, M.D., Random House, NY 1975. Dr. Feingold discovered during WWII that food additives often resulted in violent psychotic behavior and apparent "shell shock" in the military. Carrying his studies over into the child, his research has been an historic break-through. Applicable in today's rising crime rate.

Yesterday is a cancelled check,
tomorrow a promissory note,
but today is ready cash.
Each day is a beautiful gift.
—Jim Keelan, victim of the Holocaust

4. AN INCURABLE OPTIMIST

The day was perfect for the celebration. Afternoon sun glittered on the new June leaves in the park, the lawn bright and freshly mowed, and late snow still gleamed on the Colorado mountains. The audience was breathless, awaiting her entrance.

Eleanor Bliss rode into the area, her pink chiffon fluttering, sitting as straight as an arrow on her white horse, Comet. The applause thundered as the star of the show went through her paces.

The crowd cheered as Eleanor, more beautiful than ever, dismounted and made a sweeping bow, her rosy face wreathed by white hair. She was 87 years old.

The celebration was in her honor, as First Lady of Dance and the Arts. Since leaving an executive position in New York City in 1948, she has been active with the Steamboat Springs Arts Council. In 1976 she was given the Colorado Governor's Award for her contribution to the Arts and Humanities. She was the moving force in saving the abandoned railroad depot in 1972 and turning it into an Art Center, a space for art shows, and a theatre for local productions.

"Eleanor, what is the secret of your amazing vitality?"

"Well, here's one," she laughs. "Make a new young friend every day and you will never be old or alone."

That's her secret. She is always surrounded by young people, who are as natually attracted to this sparkling "young" woman as bees are to roses. It's her eternal optimism.

Life is a Celebration

Do you awake each morning with a pleasant sense of anticipation? "What unexpected adventure may occur today?" I always wonder, even before I open my eyes. That's why I always answer the telephone, no matter what I'm doing. It might be a former student in Japan, calling to offer me the gift of free airline ticket to Tokyo. Or a friend from Sweden asking me to meet her for lunch in San Francisco. It has happened. And I always expect the best.

Such constant cheerfulness drove my husband crazy. He was one of those who lived on the darker side and liked it that way. He came from a family who enjoyed the gloomier aspects of life. "Go to hell!" was sometimes his opening remark for the day, before anyone else had uttered a word — just so the world would know where he stood.

It's All in the Blood

I inherited my optimism from my father, I think. I can remember waking up in our little tar-paper shack on our Colorado homestead, to the merry strains of him singing "Give My Regards to Broadway" or "The Band Played On." He knew dozens of songs and it was a different one each day.

"It's a Great Life..."

Dad used to say, "if you don't weaken." And it was a

great life. He outlived three wives, and dropped dead one morning when he was 84. He was going to a big party that night. He loved the ladies and the ladies loved him, so he was looking forward to it, still the eternal optimist.

Happiness VS. Optimism

Beverly Sills had it all. World fame, unlimited success, and a full life. She married and had two children. One could see joy abundant in her never-failing radiance.

But in her life was tragedy, a fact which most people find hard to believe. Her little boy was mentally retarded, and her little girl was born stone deaf. Beverly Sills was broken-hearted.

"How can you be so happy, with such tragedy in your life?" she was asked.

"I'm not happy," she answered. "I am cheerful. There is a difference."

Viva la difference! Her loving optimism has repaid her a thousand times in the love and admiration showered upon her by family and friends and audiences around the world. Beverly Sills would agree with the old Chinese proverb:

> *"You cannot prevent the birds of sorrow*
> *from flying over your head,*
> *but you can prevent them*
> *from building nests in your hair."*

Grown Up at 40?

If you are, you won't have any trouble making it the rest of the way, says William Attwood in his delightful book, *Making It Through Middle Age* (Atheneum).

He faces life with verve and optimism, despite a siege

with paralytic polio, two heart attacks, a clinical depression and a near stroke — all before reaching the venerable milestone of 40. He had also changed jobs seven times, including those of foreign editor of *Look Magazine*, ambassador to Guinea, ambassador to Kenya, editor-in-chief of Cowles Communications, and president of *Newsday*, where he launched *Long Island Daily's* Sunday edition, brought up the profits 60%, and completed a $40 million plant.

"If you're really grown up by 40, you won't panic at the prospect of middle age," he says. "You'll enjoy things a lot more... and that's what life is all about, isn't it?

"There are certain advantages in growing older, like learning not to expect too much of your children, no matter what age they are. Some win prizes, some don't. Some get in trouble with the law, some don't. There's not a hell of a lot you can do about it, so why make yourself miserable?"

Having faced so many major illnesses and and come out smiling, William Attwood has become extremely aware of the body's fragility and of life's impermanence. So he steadfastly refuses to let those mysterious twinges in the neck, knees, back and elbows worry him. He advises maintaining stoic silence and realizing that most pains are transient.

"Yes, But..."

I hear someone in the back row scoff. "What if you're suffering from cancer? If it's your own life at stake, would you be so optimistic?"

Yes, if you're B. Jo Kinnick. Suffering the miseries of

the damned, following a radical mastectomy, her voice never lost that delightful "happy-days lilt" that endears her to all who know her. Although tortured by the ravages of chemotherapy, followed by pneumonia and a near-fatal attack of phlebitis, she made life sound like a great joke each time I called long-distance.

"How are you today?" I'd ask. Never once did she answer my question. Instead she responded with a patter of light-hearted insights on doctors, diseases and treatments that would have made a millionaire of any stand-up comedian. If it wasn't the medical profession she was lampooning, it was her 2-year-old grandson or their big dog, with a laugh in every line.

Through her laughter, B. Jo has conquered the enemy. Again she is commuting by bus to another city to teach poetry classes every week. And she took a cruise to Acapulco in December, cleverly scheduled between chemotherapy sessions. "The way you endure the hardships of life," someone has said, "is far more important than the hardships themselves."

It's All in Your Attitude

Recent research has proven the *physical* benefits found in a positive and cheerful *mental* attitude. The hypothalamus control center of the brain is directly connected to the immune system. If the hypothalamus gland is stimulated by cheerful attitudes, immune antibodies in the blood increase, thus strengthening the entire body. A sense of being in control of life or situations can keep stress chemicals from damaging your entire organism.

Robert Good, former president and director of

Memorial Sloan-Kettering Cancer Hospital, was one of the first doctors to point out the actual connection between the mind and the body. "A positive attitude and a constructive frame of mind," Dr. Good says, "can alter our ability to resist infections, allergies, autoimmunities or even cancer."

As someone has said, "Years wrinkle the skin, but to give up optimism wrinkles the soul."

Good reading:

Are You Happy? Dennis Wholey, New York: Houghton Mifflin, 1987. Wholey, a PBS talk-show host, interviewed dozens of people to discover if they were happy, and what made them happy.

Enthusiasms, Bernard Levin, New York: Crown Publishers, 1983. Inspiring essays by an upbeat author.

A Gift of Joy, Helen Hayes, New York: Fawcett, 1967. Beloved First Lady of American threatre quotes inspiring poetry and prose that have brought her pleasure over the years.

I Search for Rainbows, Barbara Cartland, New York: Bantam, 1977. Author of classic British romance novels, and a pioneer in the field of nutrition, reveals her optimism.

Making It Through Middle Age, William Attwood, Atheneum. A cheery look at the author's own suffering. Hope for the rest of us!

An Old Guy Who Feels Good, Worden McDonald, Berkeley: Ol'McDonald Press, 1985. Autobiography of a free-spirited working man and father of Country Joe McDonald, country singer.

The Power of Positive Thinking, Norman Vincent Peale, New York: Prentice Hall, 1952. An oldie, but still a worthwhile and reliable goodie.

Stay Alive All Your Life, Norman Vincent Peale, D.D., New York: Prentice Hall, 1957. Another excellent goodie, unharmed by age.

The kiss of the sun for pardon,
The song of the birds for mirth —
One is nearer God's heart in a garden
Than anywhere else on earth.
—Dorothy F.B. Gurney

5. IN TOUCH WITH THE EARTH

A garden is "a bit of ground that one can call his own. However small it is on the surface, it is four thousand miles deep; and that's a very handsome property," C.D. Warner wrote in 1870.

Now, with our creeks cemented over for parking lots, ticky-tacky houses climbing up over the green hills, and the wide, flower-spangled meadows covered with great industrial complexes, it is becoming increasingly impossible to find that "very handsome property."

But we *need* it! Now more than ever do we need the peace that is tangible under the open sky, with the sun hot on our backs, and our hands working the good earth. We need this communion with the source from whence we came. It restoreth the soul. Every day we work in the garden, we are rejuvenated.

4,000 Mile Roots

Whether we realize it or not, that's how deep our roots go. Clear to the center of the earth. In a way scientists can't explain, the powerful attraction of the earth for humankind is more than just an electro-magnetic force. It is the primordial attraction like that a child feels for its mother. That is why most primitive societies feel a deep reverence for "Mother Earth."

It is difficult to feel this natural affinity when you are stuck in rush-hour traffic on the freeway, or while standing in line at the supermarket, with the woman ahead having a screaming fit at the check-out clerk over her change.

Unfortunately, fewer and fewer of us are able to work in the garden for that bracing period of rejuvenation each week. The "civilized world" is creeping up on us; we are being smothered by it. That is one reason for the senseless shootings on California's freeways, I believe. Too many rats in the cage. In such hubbub, it's hard to find the roots that give us spiritual sustenance. It's sometimes difficult to remember that there is still an earth beneath us somewhere.

Go All the Way?

But some are going all the way back to Mother Earth. When he retired as cabinet-maker at the University of California Medical School Hospital in San Francisco and she as librarian in the Marin Public Schools, they packed up and moved four hours north to the red-wood country along the Eel River. The Pranges were "going back."

Louise had grown up on a big apple farm in southern Michigan, her roots deep in the earth. Spenser was a "city boy" and had no feeling for the soil. But he loved working with wood, sawing and smoothing and polishing to bring out its natural beauty, and to create something of practical value. So when they found the ugly little tumble-down shack hidden away in the woods, each of them found a challenge. And in so doing, they found themselves.

The miracles they have wrought in the past twelve years are a refreshment for the soul. Spense has turned the wreck of a cabin into a beautiful home, gleaming with wood cabinets everywhere, parquet floors, and wide picture windows that bring the north woods, with its friendly deer, into the living room. The transformation is breath-taking.

When Louise retired, she was a near-invalid with her back. She could scarcely stand, and sitting was even worse. We wondered how she would survive under the primitive conditions in a backwoods cabin.

The rejuvenation she found in returning to nature was a miracle. And the Eden she has created is a joy to behold.

They live off her vegetable garden — tomatoes, lettuce, squash, carrots, cucumbers — name it and she grows it. They've had to build ten-foot netting fences around everything to keep out the deer, who prefer her products to that found in the wild.

She also has an orchard of pears, plums, cherries, and half a dozen varieties of apples. This year our family helped with the harvest. As we picked, we sorted out the wormy apples to toss over the fence to the deer. The perfect fruit was packed in boxes to store in their basement. We all shared in the joy of harvest, exhilarated by the pull of our "4,000-mile roots."

My Aching Back!

Charles Warner wrote, "What a man needs in gardening is a cast-iron back, with a hinge in it."

But not Louise. I gaze around at the oasis she has

created in the woods and marvel, remembering the invalid she once was.

"What about your back?" I ask.

"It's 100% better than when I was a librarian!" she laughs. Her cheeks are as pink and smooth as a girl's, belying her 79 years.

"A Garden is a Lovesome Thing..."

Wrote the English poet, Thomas Brown. Sharon and Tom Young share the thought. All you have to do is visit their "plantation" in the desert of Tucson to understand.

When they bought the place in the early '70s, they wanted a home where their three children could grow up, have their school friends in, and not get in each other's way. It was a new, rambling, ranch-style house set on an acre of desert — a chaparral jungle of thorns, cactus and sand. It had two redeeming features, a swimming pool and a few baby palm trees.

You should see it today. They grow oranges, limes, lemons, tangerines, tangelos, grapefruit, peaches, pomegranates and prickly pear cactus like you wouldn't believe.

The blistering Arizona sun can scarcely find the house, now buried in a riot of bougainvillea and grape vines. The palm trees are over 50 feet high, and still growing. The place looks as though it were a part of a professional nursery. But it didn't come easy.

A Matter of Life and Death

They didn't have much time to devote to creating this desert oasis. Tom is a metallurgist and mining engineer traveling around the U.S. and abroad as a mining con-

44

sultant. Sharon is head of Quality Control at Magma Copper Company, with a daily 100-mile commute. She too does a lot of traveling in her work.

And there were three children to raise, which involved a great deal of time. When did they garden? Every spare moment!

Then tragedy struck. Tom was found to have cancer rampant throughout his whole abdominal area. The surgeon removed almost half his liver, as well as a good part of all the essential plumbing that is part of every human. Prognosis? The doctor could only shake his head. No one had ever been known to survive such extensive surgery.

But he never stopped working in the garden — whenever he could gather the strength between operations (he had three) and chemotherapy sessions. Those 4,000-mile roots into the earth continued to give him sustenance. Now it has been five years since his last chemotherapy. He is considered cured. Old Mother Earth did her share.

To Own a Bit of Ground

Rice Palmer spent some bitter 12-month winters in the desolate oil fields of Northwest Territory in Canada during WWII, dreaming of a garden. He left his heart in the Colorado mountains with his sweetheart, lovely Rosella Burbank (a relative of Luther Burbank, the horticultural genius). Her letters warmed him against the cold, while he daydreamed of their future. He had grown up on the famous old 101 Ranch in Oklahoma, owned and operated by his father. He yearned to get back to the soil.

After the war, they were married and moved to Oregon, where they bought a little house on an acreage. There Rice found his deep roots.

He became a dedicated organic gardener, and soon developed an orchard and garden that were the envy of Portland. There was not a fruit-producing tree, bush or vine that he did not cultivate in his plot. And his vegetable garden was equally spectacular. His reputation soon led him into the presidency of the Portland Organic Garden Club, where he served for several terms.

Then one day, still a young man, he had a massive heart attack. He was never again able to return to his job. However, he continued to work in his garden, "and the earth yielded up sweet fruits."

Last year Rice died at the age of 87. His ashes were placed in his garden, and over them Rosie planted a special flower, the Oklahoma rose.

$10,000 Winner

The rewards of gardening are not always merely spiritual. Have you heard the story of Alice Vonk, who had the prettiest flower garden in Sully, Iowa, a little village of less than 900 people? Since childhood, she had dreamed over the W. Atlee Burpee Co. seed catalogs every year. They usually arrived when an Iowa blizzard was howling around the eaves. Bright and colorful, they were the only indication that there would, eventually, be a spring and summer.

Alice was intrigued by one announcement that stood out among the pictures of Burpee's brilliant flowers and mouth-watering vegetables, year after year.

$10,000 Reward, it read, *to anyone who can develop a white marigold with a two-and-a-half-inch face!* For 56 years that prize dangled out there in front of Alice Vonk, who loved nothing better than gardening.

Recently she gave Burpee Seed Co. a call. "Come on over," she chirped. "I think I have it!"

In short order the head of the company, David Burpee himself, appeared at her door with his tape measure — and a check for $10,000! Today you too can enjoy Alice's lovely flower, the costliest blossom ever developed.

Your Own Roots

If you can't have your own garden, go often to a public garden where you can enjoy the rejuvenating beauty of nature. Or walk through neighborhoods where people love and tend their yards. And have a bit of nature in your own home, a geranium blooming in the window, or an ivy hanging over the kitchen sink. Keep in touch with the earth.

Good Reading:

How To Live On Less and Love It More! Jeff Cox, Rodale Press, Emmaus, PA, 1973. A guide to putting your house and grounds to work for you.

The Regeneration Garden Project, Robert Rodale, Rodale Press, Emmaus, PA 18049. An ongoing project, worldwide, for renewing the Earth, while renewing yourself. Write for information.

The Secret Life of Plants, Peter Tompkins and Christopher Bird, Harper and Row, NY, 1973. Fascinating account of the physical, emotional, and spiritual relations between plants and man.

When from our better selves we have too long
Been parted by the hurrying world, and droop,
Sick of its business, of its pleasures tired,
How gracious, how benign, is Solitude.
                                          —Wordsworth

6. THE JOY OF SOLITUDE

The Hurrying World

Sick of its business? Sick of time clocks and freeways? Of ringing phones and sordid news reports? Of bickering and pushing? Sick of people..people..people? Are you drooping, as Wordsworth wrote so many years ago? (Yes, there was too much "world" even 180 years ago.)

All this hustle and bustle is what makes a young person an old one in a hurry. If you want to avoid premature aging and early heart attacks, learn to get away from the rat race at least once a day. Learn to be alone and love it. Learn the joy of solitude.

"But how?" I hear a frazzled young mother saying. "I must get the kids and myself dressed and fed in the morning even before I get my eyes open. Get them off to school and me to work by the crack of dawn. And after a day of full-blown hassles, it's pick up the kids, stop at the supermarket for something for dinner, and dash home for a 'friendly drink' with my husband. After dinner and the kids are in bed, I'm too exhausted to do anything but set the alarm and crawl into bed, dreading the thought of its going off in the morning. Solitude? Don't be funny! When would I find any solitude?"

There are ways, strange as it may sound. Not easy to find, but they are there.

Sh!

Here is Sharon's secret. As soon as she gets home at night, she kicks off her shoes, sheds her work clothes, and locks herself in the bathroom for half an hour. No need to knock, kick the door or yell — it will do you no good. She's "off limits." She reads a few pages of a good book, or enjoys the latest issue of *Sunset* or *Sierra Club Magazine*. She comes out refreshed and relaxed, ready to prepare a leisurely dinner.

Bonnie finds her hour of solitude during her lunch break, when she takes a long, brisk walk around the university campus. Or perhaps to the pool for a few laps. And always alone. It is no help to take someone along who will chatter and keep alive the problems and pressures of work.

Put the world out of mind, and enjoy your own companionship. *Like* yourself! If you can't live with yourself, who can you live with?

Some of us live alone, out of necessity. Most of us are women, due to the immutability of mathematics. Women out-number the men in this world by a considerable majority, in numbers that increase with age. But be you men or women, there is a need to learn to *enjoy* your solitude, whether it is chosen or imposed, and to use it to your best advantage to create inner peace.

The Potty Break

As a widow living alone, I have the universal need to escape routine. My pressures are self-imposed by my own writing enthusiasm, by deadlines, by frequent interruptions, and by the responsibilities of being active in many organizations. How can I escape — when I'm already alone?

I love poetry, but for years had no time to enjoy it. I've found the solution. I keep a poetry book beside the "throne" in the bathroom. Each time I take a trip, I relax and enjoy one poem, coming out as refreshed as though coming home from a vacation in the mountains.

Solitude in a Crowd

Frank Cebulski is a technical writer at the head of his department in a big engineering firm, with nagging timetables and innumerable problems. At home he has heavy responsibilities with his three sons, a 15-year-old, a five-year-old and a one-year-old. His wife works 12-hour shifts in the intensive care unit of a big city hospital, with a two-hour commute. In addition, Frank spends many hours each week with his older son, coaching both his soccer and baseball teams. Many was the time he carried the baby in a back-pack while out on the field, coaching his team. He was always running dangerously behind schedule in everything, as he rushed breathlessly from one responsibility to another. Where can such a man find his necessary solitude?

Coffee break! But instead of taking it in the lounge area with the other employees, Frank slips out of his high-rise office building and across the street to a sidewalk cafe. There, for a blessed 15 minutes, he is alone, even with the noisy hubbub of city traffic and pedestrians milling about him. He does not hear it, for he is writing a poem.

He has had two books of poetry published.

If you *like* yourself, you will be able to slip off to have a quiet rendezvous with your best friend (yourself) when you need it. Even in a crowded city, there are ways. I suspect that this is one reason we see so many joggers on city streets, their ears muffled with Walkman earphones, their eyes glazed by distance. They aren't really here at all. They are escaping to solitude, insulated by music.

Urban Wilderness

It is easy to be stifled by the noisy tumult of a city, especially an overgrown, overcrowded, over-skyscrapered city like New York. Bonnie is "allergic" to crowds, and although she had a busy schedule in the Big Apple, she felt she had to break out of the closeness of a million people.

Before the sun burned off the mists of Manhattan, she was in Central Park, walking the nearly empty paths. Suddenly face to face she met a jogger, someone she recognized from her days in Steamboat Springs, when he had attended Perry-Mansfield School of Theatre. She remembered him once whispering to his hostess there, "I'm going now, Miss Smith. I'm allergic to parties." It was Dustin Hoffman!

The Highest Mountain

John Muir wrote, "Climb the mountains and get their good tidings. Nature's peace will flow into you as sunshine flows into trees. The winds will flow their freshness into you, and the storms their energy, while cares drop off like storm leaves."

7. MAKE LIFE A WINDOW

"Perhaps I should warn you that I am not an *average* senior citizen, if there is such a thing," I wrote to Charles Inlander, president of the People's Medical Society, in response to a request for answers on how to live long. "After an exhilarating career in education around the world, I quit at 60 to go back to school, earn a master's degree in play writing, and take up a new career. In the past 15 years, I have had four books of poetry, a novel, and two biographies published. This week I mailed a new biographical novel to my agent and am clearing my desk to start the next book."

My advice on living long was: "Make life a window, not a mirror. Look out at others. Avoid looking in, brooding over yourself. Don't join the 'Me Generation.' "

I was delighted when Mr. Inlander saw fit to publish the above in *People's Medical Society Health Bulletin*, "Living Long by People Who Have."

Think of your most interesting friends. Why do you like to be with them? Are their minds turned "in" on themselves, on their own troubles? Do they entertain you with an "organ recital" of their ailments? Or are they more interested in looking "out" at the world around them? Are they more excited about events in Hong Kong and the people "out there" than they are about their own problems?

Notice: No Organ Recital Today!

Post those words over your doorbell, inked in bright red. Promise yourself you will steer clear of the subject of your health. Instead try some light-hearted conversation, and see if those aches and pains don't fade away.

Cleone Montgomery taught me that magic. She was in either a wheelchair or a hospital bed the last ten years of her life. She spent the last five years in a mediocre "rest home," a misnomer if there ever was one. A beloved friend when she was well and strong, she remained one until her death at the age of 96. I loved going to see her. She was always good for a laugh and never once did she complain of anything. (And she had plenty to complain about.) She had thrown away the mirror. She was interested in *you*.

A Very Small House

"I live in a very small house," wrote Confucius, "but my windows look out on a very large world."

Ramayeo Yeomans lives in a very small house in Carmel, California, a tiny three-room cottage almost lost in the shadows of the towering pines. Ramayeo is 97, and she has brought 97 years of the great outside world into that small house.

Her bright eyes sparkle as she answers your questions about the beautiful pieces of sculpture you see everywhere — all her own work. She has been a talented sculptor since she studied with the famous Dorothea Denslow at Perry-Mansfield School in the early '20s. Most of her work, she admits, she has given away.

"He was a friend of mine," she says, gently touching a statue of an American Indian, a man with a strong god-like face. "Netzahault. A wonderful man."

There is another statue, a graceful Hindu girl surrounded by animals.

"That's Ahimsa," says Ramayeo. "Ahimsa means non-violence toward all life. This is my gesture against vivisection and cruelty to animals, which I've worked against all my life.

"My most important statue is of the Peace Pilgrim. That amazing women who walked over 25,000 miles to promote world peace. When I heard that Peace Pilgrim was coming through my little town of Brandon in Canada, I got on my bicycle and went out to meet her. I invited her home to spend a few days with me, and we became fast friends. In her book she wrote, 'I shall remain a wanderer until mankind has learned the ways of peace.' I made a statue of her and gave it to the Peace Pilgrim Center in Hemet in Southern California.

"Here's something I want you to have," and she hands you a little book, *The Hundredth Monkey*, by Ken Keyes.

"I've sent that to heads of state all over the world. It's a legend about planetary peace. I've had letters from the President of Mexico and of France, from Prime Minister Trudeau, and from Carl Sagan. Now there's a wonderful man!" she interrupts herself.

"Do you know what it says about war in the UNICEF charter? 'War begins in the minds of men. Since this is so, the minds of men must be capable of ending war.' "
(Courtesy of The Sunday Herald, Carmel, CA.)

See what I mean? A visit with Ramayeo leaves you full

of enthusiasm for life. If she suffers from some of the maladies of age, it's not the focus of her life. She's too busy looking out the window.

Bristols' Window

Everett and Benita Bristol were a remarkable couple who lived all their lives in the little mountain town of Steamboat Springs, Colorado. But the wall of mountains around the valley in no way hemmed them in. Nearing retirement age, they looked back on a long career of public service in their community. As an engineer with the local Rural Electrification Administration, Everett spent many months in various under-developed countries around the world, helping them get electrification projects under way.

When I wrote asking for a few notes on their latest adventure, I got a fascinating account from Ev, handwritten, with a covering letter saying they were off soon for another overseas assignment, two months in the Middle East to help bring electricity to North Yemen.

The Bristols didn't merely make life a window. They made it a door, and walked out to meet it more than halfway. But Ev's story is so splendid, I must share it with you:

"Benita and I have long been fascinated by distant lands, different cultures and especially the small kingdom of Nepal...But when could we go? A sudden death in the family answered the question for us — don't put off doing the things you really want to do!

"So, in a short time, we were on our way: Steamboat-Denver-Seattle-Tokyo-Bangkok-Kathmandu. Total trip covered 30 days, 19 of which were spent trekking.

"Despite proper warning and ample advice, we nevertheless hired a young Sherpa guide 'off the street' near our guest house in Kathmandu. Our 'good vibes' were well-founded and we enjoyed a most pleasant three weeks with our guide and porters.

"Our trek out of Pokhara took us in five days to the base camp in the Annapurna Sanctuary, and another five days as far as Kalponi on the Jamosom trail. We were blessed with beautiful weather, leech-free following the summer monsoons, and warm except for the nights in the Sanctuary. There at 13,000 feet, our tents were ice-covered, frozen stiff each morning, but it melted off during the brief hours of daily sunshine.

"Our sincere efforts to 'get in shape' before we left for Nepal were helpful, but still inadequate. The first three days we were totally exhausted — alternately climbing steep ridges and dropping sharply to the valley floors. The toil and sweat, and change of diet (no meat during the 19 days) equalled a weight loss of a pound per day! We were endlessly amazed at the skill of the small-statured Sherpas in negotiating the steep, rocky trails and treacherous stream crossing, burdened by 35-50 kilo loads. How do they do it?

"Rewards aplenty fulfilled our dreams and expectations. Standing at 14,000 feet we craned our necks sharply to gaze up at yet another two miles vertical to the Annapurna peaks surrounding us.

"Each evening in a tea house or at a campsite was a delight. Chatting with fellow trekkers from all corners of the world, sharing experiences of the day and weeks past, and plans of future destinations, created bonds of kinship. And, would you believe, on the trail in the far reaches of Nepal, acquaintances from our own small hometown? Small world?"

Shortly after their return, Ev died of cancer. But what a life! All of it a window open to the world.

Never Be Bored

Erma Bombeck says, "It's sad somehow that the No. 1 malady in this country is boredom." How true. Ten years ago my small granddaughter was saying, "I'm bored." And now it's my next grandchild with the same theme, "I'm bored."

"Don't ever let anyone hear you say that!" I told them. "What you really mean when you say that is 'I'm boring.' The world is full of thousands of things to get excited about, and if you don't get excited about them, it's because you're too dull and boring to look around you."

Last night I met an exciting young woman at a dinner meeting of the Woman's National Book Association. She was very beautiful, made even more so by her lively enthusiasm about her new profession, writing children's books. She appeared to be college age, so I was amazed to learn that she was a lawyer, writing legal text books, and doing the children's books on the side.

Then I noticed that both hands were cruelly distorted by degenerative arthritis. If there was anyone who might be expected to be home, moaning in self-pity, she would be the one. Instead she was enjoying herself immensely, while her dinner companions were enjoying her!

There's no good excuse for being bored. If you're an invalid, read! I had a friend many years ago who became gradually bedfast with multiple sclerosis. She read until she was unable to hold a book. I got her a reading stand that stood up on legs and held the book above her body.

At last she could no longer turn the pages, but occasionally her young son would come in to turn a page for her.

But was she ever bored — or boring? Not that anyone ever noticed. She was always cheerful, looking out her "window" into the world outside her bedroom, eager to discuss the latest book.

Browse! Libraries are a veritable treasure-house of excitement. I get so inspired doing research in the endless stacks at the library of UC Berkeley, I lose all sense of time and place. One Friday night, in fact, I was locked in the stacks at closing time and didn't realize it until an hour later. I had to take off my shoe and break the glass of the fire alarm with my heel before I could escape.

You don't need to be entertained. Entertain yourself.

Look Out

Open the windows of your life. Look at people, at flowers, at buildings (old and new), in museums and art galleries, at shopwindows, clothes, antique shops, historical markers, sunsets, stars, trees, mountains, insects, pets. Everything you see can set your imagination afire. It's a great big, beautiful, wonderful world out there!

Don't waste your time superimposing your own image over everything you see. Those who do (and their number is legion), see only a dark image, blurred and obscured by the ugly ghost of self-pity.

Comparing one's self to everyone else is destructive. If you consider yourself superior to others, you appear arrogant and rude. If you consider yourself inferior, you seem paranoid and self-pitying. Neither is conducive to lasting friendships nor pleasant conversation.

Some people carry around on their backs a lifelong "sack" of past hurts, injustices and grudges, where they will always have them handy to bring out and polish up. It becomes a great burden, this "sad sack." If you have one, throw it away. Don't cling to those misfortunes. Everyone has them. Yours are not so special. Why not look out the window at the rest of the world?

*A happy man or woman is a
radiant focus of goodwill and
their entrance into a room is as
though another candle has been lighted.*
—Robert Louis Stevenson

8. LOOK GOOD!

You Can Be Beautiful

Beauty is not necessarily what you were born with. It is what you develop as you mature. It is a strange and somewhat intangible combination of elements which are totally within your power to develop, either consciously or unconsciously. Some are internal, some are external. But they are yours to make the most of.

When Ruth Greffenius walks into a room, conversation stops. Heads turn. Who is this tall, regal-looking blonde?

She has an aura about her that is hard to define. Part of it is her figure and posture. She walks tall and with easy grace. Part of it is her grooming. Hair is always beautifully done. Make-up so subtle that it is invisible. Is she wrinkled? I don't know. I never noticed. I just know that the animation in her lovely face sweeps everything else out of mind. She is interested, interesting and exciting.

Are her clothes fashionable? I can't remember, although I saw her only last week. I do know that she looks like a fashion plate at all times, chic outfits that suit her gracious style, and do not shout for attention.

But it is not her facade that lights up the room. It is an inner radiance, a sense of perfect self-assurance, and a dramatic flare that comes from years working in community theatre. She knows who she is, and then doesn't give her looks another thought.

The courtly bearing of her tall dark husband, Griff, is a perfect foil. A strikingly handsome couple. The applause was overwhelming at their golden wedding celebration as they skimmed across the dance floor, looking like a 1940s movie of the king and queen of some unnamed European monarchy.

When their children took to the floor behind them, then grandchildren, and finally the great-grandchildren, the applause swelled to the rafters.

The Way We See Ourselves

"Our grooming and appearance affect not only how others perceive us, they affect the way we feel about ourselves," says Dr. Joyce Brothers, the attractive TV personality.

"When we feel we look good, our self-esteem grows. Our increased self-esteem lifts our confidence, improves our performance, and, in turn, favorably affects what others think of us and how they behave toward us.

"Good grooming, exercise, nutrition, hygiene and other practices that contribute to good appearance," continues Dr. Brothers, "do more than improve psychological well-being and boost confidence. They offer immediate tangible and practical benefits.

"Well-groomed job applicants are chosen more often and offered higher salaries that less well-groomed rivals. Once in their jobs, they are more likely to be promoted and have their salary increased.

"The most obvious benefit of good grooming and attention to personal appearance is increased sexual allure. The appeal of a bright smile, pleasant fragrance, healthy hair, and clear complexion has probably created more advertising, sold more goods and services, and produced more economic activity than any other urge man has or will ever want. If sexual appeal were the only benefit good grooming conferred, many would consider their effort well spent."

Take What You Have and Run

Many of us are not endowed with special good looks, unusual talents, or indeed, anything extraordinarily attractive or appealing. Some of us are even burdened with personal irregularities which, when we're young, may seem to be insurmountable handicaps and ugliness.

I was one of those people, and I know, from years of self-abasement and embarrassment, what difficulties these youngsters face. I had six — not one but six — irregularities of which I was hideously ashamed.

1. I was fat, and had been since infancy.
2. I had a severe case of scoliosis (curvature of the spine) which required specially made clothes.
3. My third deformity was an enlarged abdomen, due to "too much gut," as one doctor inelegantly put it (a genetic defect). He proposed surgery, but I declined.
4. I had bosoms that would riveal Dolly Parton's. Fashionable in the '90s, but in the flat flapperish '20s they were positively obscene. I kept

my arms clutched across my chest, hoping to conceal my natural endowments.

5. My hip bones were spaced wide, a dandy setup for producing babies, but hardly a popular feature for the college coed of the '30s.
6. I had practically no waistline, as my hips were contiguous to my ribs, making the wearing of belts an impossiblity.

But despite all this, I somehow endured my youth, found a husband who didn't seem to mind my imperfect figure, had two lovely daughters, and learned to dress in a way that concealed, to a great extent, my irregularities. In other words, I learned to take what I had and run with it!

You Needn't Be Perfect

You can create an illusion of pleasant normality by good grooming, becoming clothes, and an inner peace and joy. What's inside can often camouflage a faulty exterior. Lighted windows at night can give a gracious effect of warmth to a tumble-down house.

A dear young friend sent me this birthday card last year:

"Wrinkles are God's little way of saying...'I'm stepping on your face.' " He has certainly made some deep tracks on mine in the past 79 years, but I don't really mind. I tell myself that those wrinkles are the hieroglyphics recording the marvelously exciting life I have lived on four continents.

Keep Your Weight Down

"Pot bellies" are the plague of many of us during our older years. Dorothy T., 80, and weighing in at very little more than that, worried about her "fat tummy." So did Charlotte P., an angular woman and vigorous dancer who was athletic up into her 90s. Both worried about "getting fat." Nonsense! Geriatric specialists tell us that the extra padding on the tummy is nature's way of conserving body heat in our vital organs, by blanketing them with a safety layer of fat. This "pot belly syndrome" is augmented by the weakening of abdominal muscles with advancing years, allowing gravity to do its darnedest, as it does with a sagging face. Don't worry about it. But a good daily stint of walking will help by tightening tummy muscles.

Be sure you aren't carrying around an extra ruck-sack full of fat. Check with a weight chart or with your doctor to see if you are burdened by an overload of fat. That will make an old person (or even a corpse) of you in a hurry.

Losing weight isn't really so difficult, if you go at it the right way. (I've tried all ways, most of them wrong, until I found the secret.) Cut out the fat and sugar! Pasta is great for the diet, provided you omit all fat. It's fat that makes you fat. Pasta satisfies hunger and fills you up. So does a fresh green salad, without regular salad dressing. Make your own dressing with nonfat yogurt and salad spices. Chicken (without skin) and fish, broiled without fat, and plenty of fresh vegetables will complete the diet. You need never go hungry.

And the final part of the secret: walking! Walk briskly at least a mile a day — every day. And you'll lose those extra pounds. I guarantee it! I did it.

Sexy Feet

One of the hallmarks of a chic sophisticated woman seems to be trim ankles and high heels. But gorgeous gams don't always mean a gorgeous face. Those sexy shoes may be what etches the deep furrows of pain in an otherwise attractive face. Some women will suffer agonies to "be beautiful," not realizing that they are piling on quick lines of aging with fashionable shoes.

I marvel at the ultra chic women of Paris, tapping along the boulevards on four-inch spike heels. Beautiful, yes, until you look into their faces, pinched and angry with pain. I spent some weeks in Paris not long ago, doing intensive research for the book I was writing. I was on my feet for long days, trudging from one source of information to another. At first I was a bit embarrassed to be seen striding around in my flat rubber-soled walking shoes. But with the miles I was putting in, I knew I couldn't have done it in heels.

At home I live in tennis shoes. I can walk miles in them, and come home smiling. I attribute a great proportion of my "eternal youth" to comfortable feet.

Smile, Darn You, Smile

The best work-out you can give sagging face muscles is the "smile exercise" — about 12 hours a day. Ever notice how crabby older people look when they allow gravity to have its way? All the lines go down. Jowls develop. The mouth turns down at the corners. One or two frowns settle in, turning the brows downward toward the nose.

Stand in front of your mirror and laugh at that grouchy mug. Aren't you ridiculous? Then, suddenly, something miraculous happens. All the lines turn up! And in that up turning, you drop off at least a dozen years. Try it and see.

This "laugh phenomenon" works two ways: first, by pulling up the sagging muscles, and secondly, by calling in the endorphins, your body's natural pain killers. This gives your face a more youthful, attractive appearance.

In Praise of Older Women — and Men

It has long been a fact that young women often prefer older men as escorts, lovers and husbands. A well-groomed grey-haired man is distinguished, attractive. A bald head does not detract from a man's sex appeal, if he is charming and more interested in others than in himself. Personal grooming is often the difference between an attractive male and a seedy, run-down "old man."

Now, it seems, older women are coming into their own, too. Not long ago *Harper's Bazaar* published a list of America's most beautiful women, among them Lena Horne, 70; Candice Bergen, 41; Diahann Carrol, 52; Faye Dunaway, 47; Ali MacGraw, 47; and Elizabeth Taylor, 56. For years the French have had a rich tradition of loving older women. And now America is catching on. More older women are becoming involved with younger men, who find they have far more to offer than many blank-faced (and blank-minded) girls. Not to worry. These girls will improve with age.

Age has nothing to do with how attractive a person is. Barbara Cartland, Princess Di's step-grandmother and England's most prolific romance writer, has long held that good looks and good health go hand in hand. One of Britain's most beautiful women for many decades, she was one of the world's earliest and most fervent proselytizers for good nutrition and vitamin supplements. Now she is the living proof.

It's in Your Head

Marian Diamond is most often seen with the model of a human brain in her hands. This strikingly beautiful woman, exquisitely dressed and groomed, appears to be about 40. In reality she is 63, and was recently chosen the "Professor of the Year" at Cal Berkeley, placing third in the national competition for that title.

Prof. Diamond is a neuro-anatomist, and has been researching the human brain and its relation to nutrition for the past 40 years. Her conclusions?

A healthy, long-lived brain (and consequently the person owning it) depends on four factors: 1) *Activity.* "Too many people give up because they've been told they should start going downhill at 40. Keep active, mentally and physically. 2) *A healthy diet.* The alert people she interviewed in their 80s and 90s all drank milk and ate eggs. Those who didn't, she found becoming senile. 3) *Good genes.* Of the over 10,000 people in the US today who are over 100, most probably owe it largely to parents who also lived long lives. 4) *A purpose. "Having a purpose is terribly important."* Professor Joel Hildebrand at UC Berkeley is one of her shining examples. He walked up four flights of stairs to his laboratory every day until he died at 101. "He enjoyed his chemistry, which gave him something to look forward to each day. The joy of discovery kept him going. He's the epitome of what we are trying to show can occur in the brain in optimum conditions."

Beauty Is From the Inside

When Sophia Loren, 54, was interviewed on TV recently she was asked what her beauty secret was...does she exercise, does she have a special diet? What is her magic?

"You're surprised I look good?" she laughed.

"You don't look good. You look fabulous! There's a big difference!"

"I have a very positive attitude," she answered thoughtfully. "I like myself. I feel good inside my skin. There is no magic."

There is the magic! Feel good about yourself. Feel good about the world around you. Joy in life ignites a flame inside you. The glow that inner flame is called beauty.

"As artists know, if there is anything behind a face, that face improves with age," says Kare De Crow, former president of NOW. "Lines show distinction and character: they show that one has lived."

Good luck! You'll look better tomorrow.

But in ourselves, are triumph or defeat.
—Henry Wadsworth Longfellow

9. COPING WITH STRESS

Stress kills more people than cancer and heart attacks combined. More doctors and scientists are coming to this conclusion every day. In fact, they are becoming convinced that stress is one of the causative factors in both these diseases which end in death. But what we are more concerned with here is that stress speeds up the aging process rapidly and irreparably, unless we can find some way to cope.

There's no question that today's world is becoming more stressful by the minute. Just watching the evening news for a week will bring up your blood pressure to the danger zone — unless you can develop a satisfactory way to cope. Just commuting to work through the rush hour traffic is enough to put you in the hospital — and often does. Today's highly advanced (?) society is rapidly becoming Dante's inferno.

Learning to cope is your only solution. Keeping yourself youthful, vigorous, and optimistic is the first step toward a better world for everyone. You can't solve any external problems until you can solve your own.

Music — A Prescription for Health?

> *This music crept by me upon the waters,*
> *Allaying both their fury, and my passion,*
> *With its sweet air.*   —Shakespeare

Shakespeare seems to be talking about today's "new age" music, a product of the '80s. Scientists are discovering that stress can often be controlled through the ears, strange as it may seem. Steven Halpern, Ph.D., author and composer of "anti-frantic" music, has discovered through research that the pulse rate can actually be controlled through the beat of music. A group of nurses, monitoring their own pulses, found that their pulse rate was lowered or raised with a change of rhythm.

Traditional music rises to a climax, bringing the tension of the listener to a peak along with it, Halpern says. "New-age" music, now available in most record stores, flows along smoothly through a variety of sounds, sometimes with sounds of nature, the wind, the sea, and sometimes with sweet electronic melody. It is a non-obtrusive kind of music, music you can work to, or relax to, or even sleep to, cutting out bothersome and disagreeable background sounds.

Life is Like an Ice Cream Cone

Charles Schulz, delightful philosopher and creator of the popular *Peanuts* comic strip, says, "Life is like an ice cream cone. You have to learn to lick it."

Stress or Distress?

Dr. Hans Selye, the world's foremost authority on stress, published a book entitled *Stress Without Distress*. In it he said, "Complete freedom from stress is death! Don't try to avoid stress — it's the very salt and spice of life. But do learn to master and use it."

Dr. Selye urges people — especially older people — to find some kind of life where they can *win*. It's the frustration of never being able to achieve goals that causes dis-tress.

70

Dr. Selye says that there are two kinds of stress — distress (from *dis* meaning bad as in disaster) and eustress (*eu* meaning good, as in euphoric). You can't avoid stress—and indeed, you don't want to. But the eustress does no harm, and is even beneficial. Think of how many people you know who lead highly stressful lives and thrive on it.

Consider the fact that Oliver Wendell Holmes, who fought in some of the bloodiest battles of the Civil War, was discharged for total exhaustion, and went on to a career almost as stressful as Chief Justice of the Supreme Court. Yet he lived to a hale and hearty 94. Why? Unlike his Civil War experience, his Supreme Court stresses were exciting, challenging — in other words, eustress, not distress.

Be a Willow, Not a Pine

The Japanese have an adage, "Be a willow, not a pine." In others words, bend with the storm, don't fight it and you will survive, like the willow. The pine tree refuses to bend, and it is shattered.

Dr. Selye learned this lesson when he was a child. Be adaptable. "I pride myself on being able to adapt myself to almost everything that has ever happened to me," he says.

In 1972 Dr. Selye discovered that he had reticulosasarcoma, the most malignant cancer known, fatal in 99.5% of cases. What should he do? Whimper away the last year of his life? Or squeeze the best possible living into that final year? He chose the latter. Lo and behold — a strange thing happened. A year passed, and another, and another, with Selye living the fullest, most fulfilling life possible, as was his custom. He lived another 10 years.

"Sloan-Kettering Institute," Dr. Selye said, "found that when people truly want to live, they make a greater effort and their immunization somehow works better... The great majority of physical illnesses have in part some psychosomatic origin." And learning to adapt, to accept his cancer and still live life to the hilt, was his triumph in learning to cope.

What's the Use of Worrying?

Some people are dedicated worriers. It's their hobby. Even their vocation. It gives them something to do, something to talk about. I once had a beloved friend, God rest her soul, who was one of the most proficient worriers of all time.

"Worrying never solved anything," I used to reason with her. "If you have a problem, it either has a solution — or it hasn't. If you can do something about it — find a solution — do it. If you can't, forget it, and get on with your life. Stewing about it doesn't do you, or anyone else, any good."

But she continued to worry until she died an early death.

Scientists now list worry and indecision high on the list of stress factors. I am often too quick and impetuous in my decisions, but I hate fussing and fretting and wavering to such an extent that I will gladly change my mind later, if necessary, and without regrets. It's healthier that way.

I like this story from *Modern Maturity*: When the centenarian was asked the secret of his long life, he replied, "When I work, I work easy. When I sit, I sit loose. When I start to worry, I go to sleep."

As Scarlett O'Hara would say when she came to a difficult problem in *Gone With The Wind*, "I'll worry about that tomorrow."

Tips from The American Institute of Stress

Here are a few solutions to stress which I have adapted from the studies of Paul J. Rosch, M.D., president of this prestigious organization.

Get away from it all. I prefer flight to fight. Get away from the battle scene for awhile, while the air clears.

Surround yourself with friends. Have at least one friend with a shoulder to cry on when the going gets tough.

Don't let finances ruin you. Money, or the lack of it, or how to spend it has ruined more good marriages than any other cause. Work out a sensible plan in advance. Don't just drift into bankruptcy. Don't spend more than you earn. Don't buy anything until you can pay cash.

Cool it. If you're angry or upset, don't let yourself go. Keep the lid on. Keep your voice down... and...gentle. Escape until your anger cools. Then you can discuss it with happier results.

Toss out "problems." Eradicate that word from your vocabulary. Substitute "challenge" instead.

Never say "must." Get rid of the nagging words "I must, I should." They magnify your stress (and distress).

Don't think negative thoughts. I like the old saying, "You can't keep trouble from calling, but you needn't offer it a chair."

Don't worry about little things. As Dr. Robert Elliot, a cardiologist from the University of Nebraska says, "Don't sweat the small stuff — and remember it's all small stuff."

Laugh! Northern California residents get their a laugh-a-day from the *Chronicle* columnist, Herb Caen. One of my favorite "Caenites" is "All you need in life is one great shining delusion. Mae West firmly believed she was 20 until she was well into her 80s and then she died happily, never suspecting her mistake."

Family ties. Give them a chance to bind. Many people scarcely know what their own family believes, thinks or wants. In trying to give their children everything, they are missing the boat on the most important element of all, their own time.

"The good life" may not be the best. Ever stop to think what all that extra work to reach the top rung really gets you? A beautiful home and all the luxuries. Great! But it also means more work, more commuting time to work, more bills — and an early heart attack. Why not settle for less?

Lead a double life. Keep your life compartmentalized. During my 40 years of teaching, I led two distinct lives, each with enthusiasm. I never brought school work or problems home, nor home problems to school. I was two separate people — a wonderful way to cut stress in half..

Moderation. Although a dull, middle-of-the-road word, it's worth more than its weight in diamonds! Stick to moderation in all things, working, playing, eating, drinking. Overdoing in any of these, even though perhaps euphoric at the time, brings on stress (and early aging).

Make home a place to relax. Make your living room a warm, cozy place where friends can curl up to talk. Not a show place, like Grandmother's front parlor, where everyone was afraid to spread out for fear of messing up the antimacassars and what-nots. Your kitchen can be another bright haven, where family and friends can gather for chatter, popcorn and laughter, or just watch you cook.

Get cooperation with the housework. Everyone in our family had a share in making the home a clean, hospitable attractive gathering place for friends of all ages, students, lonely bachelors, unwed teachers, Grandma and Grandpa, and foreign students from around the world. This was only possible by everyone's pitching in to help make our place a home.

Don't try to be perfect. Who really cares if there's dust on the buffet and smudges on the kitchen cupboards, if the family is happily gathered around the table?

Don't forget that smile. The American Institute of Stress says that there's something about a smile that helps you cope with any problem. Smile big — and crack a joke. It's cheaper, quicker, and healthier than a tranquilizer.

Biofeedback Can Do the Trick

Modern technology has one invention that is priceless in helping you cope with stress. After my husband died, I became a basket case. My health had disintegrated during the long months beside his hospital bed, watching him leave us. After my daughter talked me out of suicide, I decided to try biofeedback. The young doctor shook hands when I walked into his office.

"Your blood pressure is very high," he said immediately.

"How can you tell?" I asked in amazement. I'd seen him for no more than three seconds.

"Your hands are icy cold, a dead give-away," he laughed. Then he told me to relax in a big chair there and to picture the capillaries in my fingers slowly enlarging and allowing the blood to flow easily, warming my hands. Any imagery I wanted to use was fine. But before we began, he taped tiny thermometers to my fingers and fastened equipment to my head and hands resembling that used in doing an electrocardiogram. I was wired to an instrument with dials, beepers, and lights. I could see and hear if I was on the right track, or if I was tensing up again. Then he left me to go it alone.

Fifteen minutes later he was back. It had worked. The temperature of my fingers had risen several degrees. He took my blood pressure, which had dropped amazingly. "How did I do it?" I asked, totally astonished.

"You got the right idea in a hurry," he grinned. "What imaging did you use?"

"I was in a summer meadow of yellow flowers," I admitted, slightly embarrassed.

"Some people have to come back repeatedly for quite a period of time. But I think you've got it. Just keep up the good work at home."

Help To Cope with Stress:

Alcoholics and Alcoholism, Harvy Milt, Scientific Aids
   Publications, Fair Haven, NJ, 1968

Alcoholism: A Merry-Go-Round Named Denial,
   Al-Anon Family Group, NY

Alex -The Life of a Child, Frank Deford. Cystic Fibrosis
   Foundation, P.O. Box 17105, Baltimore, MD 21203.
   Arrangement with New American Library and Viking
   Press, 1983. The unforgettable story of a courageous
   little girl's battle for life against cystic fibrosis.

American Institute of Stress, 124 Park Avenue, Yonkers, NY
   10703. Excellent source of information for anti-stress.

Conquering Pain, Dr. Sampson Lipton, Arco Publishing, NY,
   1984. How to overcome the discomforts of arthritis,
   backache, migraine, heart disease, childbirth, period
   pain and many other common conditions.

Feel The Fear—And Do It Anyway, Susan Jeffers, Ph.D.,
   Fawcett Columbine, NY, 1987. Dynamic techniques for
   turning fear, indecision and anger into power, action,
   and love.

Courage is a three-Letter Word, Walter Anderson. Fawcett
   Crest, 1986. How many distinguished Americans have
   overcome their fears.

*Exercises for the Parkinson Patient, With Hints for Daily
   Living*, Lucien Coté, MD and Georgia Riedel, RPT of
   Columbia University Department of Rehabilitation
   Medicine. Parkinson's Disease Foundation, Columbia
   University Medical Center, 650 W. 168th St., NY 10032.
   Write for information.

Generation to Generation, Tom Owen-Towle, Sunflower Ink
   Books, Carmel, 1985. Passing along the good life to
   your children. Brings power and hope to parents and
   children alike.

*Hopeful Living: How to Put Regeneration to Work in Your
   Life*, Robert Rodale. Rodale Press, Emmaus, PA, 1987.
   Practical ways to regenerate your life on the road to
   health and happiness.

Leaving the Office Behind, Barbara Mackoff, Ph.D., P.G.
Putnam Sons, NY, 19845. Wise ways to avoid many of
today's stresses.

Life After Harry, Virginia Graham, Simon and Schuster, NY,
1988. A widow shares the challenges of widowhood,
showing how to make a successful transition from two
to one.

The Relaxation Response, Herbert Benson, M.D., Avon Books
and Wm. Morrow and Co. Dr. Benson, Associate
Professor of Medicine at the Harvard Medical School
gives priceless advice on conquering stress.

Stop Stress and Aging Now, Dr. David C. Gardner and Dr.
Grace Joely Beatty. American Training and Research
Associates, Inc. Publishers, 1985. The 3% formula for
staying young, healthy and sexy, by spending 3% of
your time through meditation (relaxation), correct diet,
and vitamin supplements.

Stresscare Systems, Inc., 1000 Northern Blvd., Great Neck,
NY 11021. A good place to write for help in coping
with widowhood.

Stress Without Distress, Dr. Hans Selye. New American
Library, NY, 1974. How to use stress for your own
advantage, by the world's foremost authority on stress.

Stress Management Seminars,, Dr. and Mrs. Jerome G.
Downing, Star Route 3374, Woodland Park, CO 80863.
(719)687-6218. This dynamic couple flies all over the
US giving stress seminars.

*To Live Again: Rebuilding Your Life After You've Become a
Widow*, Genevieve Davis Ginsberg, M.S., St. Martins
Press, 1987. Invaluable day-to-day advice on the
process of putting your life back together after the loss
of a spouse.

Grow old along with me!
The best is yet to be,
The last of life, for which the first was made.
—Robert Browning

10. THE LAST HALF IS BEST

What's Left After 50?

Plenty, honey! Plenty! Don't let a little thing like 50 candles on your cake flip you into a state of suicidal depression. You may have the city fire department roaring in with sirens screaming when you blow out all those candles, but for heaven's sake, don't be depressed! Enjoy the fun!

Take Robert Browning, the 19th century English poet, as a case in point. He had every reason to be depressed when he wrote the above quotation. He had just lost his beloved wife, Elizabeth Barrett, leaving him bereft and alone with a small son to bring up. Browning, 49, broke up his household in Florence, where he and Elizabeth had spent 15 years after their romantic elopement. Returning to England, he settled in the ugliest part of London. Poets have never been known for their wealth. A pretty bleak outlook for a man facing the last half of his life. Right?

The first thing he did after settling into his grubby neighborhood was to gather all his poetry together into three volumes, which he had no difficulty in getting published. Gradually he began to get the upper hand of his crushing loss. He started writing again with tremendous drive and fecundity.

"Everybody wished him to come and dine," wrote

Mr. Sharp, a biographer of the time, "and he did his utmost to gratify everybody...He read all the notable books; kept acquainted with the leading contents of journals and magazines; conducted a large correspondence, read new French, German and Italian books; translated Euripides and Aschylus; knew all the gossip of the literary clubs, salons and studios; was a frequenter of afternoon tea parties; and then, over and above it, he was Browning," England's most beloved poet since Shakespeare (from *Browning's Complete Poems*, Houghton Mifflin, 1895). Despite all this attention from London society, he still continued to turn out reams of poetry.

Browning died at the ripe age of 77, while visiting his artist son in Venice. How prophetic his own words, "Grow old along with me, the best is yet to be," written at 49.

What Is Left After Retirement?

Let me tell you the true story of a man who retired, willingly or not, at the customary retirement age. Pestered by the usual aches and pains of advancing maturity, he tried to look forward with pleasure to a life of total ease, but he failed to find much joy in the prospect. All his life he had worked under tremendous pressures, and a future with nothing more challenging than making the choice of which shirt to put on each morning left him chilled and depressed. He had been too busy during his career to develop any absorbing hobbies, and so now here he was, an "old man," put out to pasture, with nothing to do.

And then the Japanese dropped the bomb on Pearl

Harbor. He went back to work full tilt. He was needed, and that knowledge lent sudden youth to his step. His aches and pains evaporated into thin air. Back in the old job once again, he was now given assignments with stresses that would have destroyed a much younger man (he was now 62).

He was made commander of the Allied Forces in the Southwest Pacific and directed the campaign against New Guinea. He freed the Philippines from the Japanese and then accepted the official surrender of the Japanese on board the U.S.S. Missouri on September 2, 1945. That man, of course, was five-star general Douglas MacArthur, who went on to direct the reconstruction of Japan, and later, to command the UN forces in the Korean War. By that time, he was a man in his 70s.

But today it is not as a warrior that he is widely revered in Japan, but as a peace-maker, the man who brought Western thought and democracy to the Land of the Rising Sun, who guided them in writing their constitution and in leading them into the 20th century.

This gratitude is given tangible evidence in the majestic and handsomely pillared building in Tokyo in front of which sits a bronze statue of MacArthur — The MacArthur Memorial. And this, because of what he accomplished *after* retirement!

Runaway Best Seller

Americans are not the only people who are looking into the goals of growing older with panache. The Japanese are gung-ho for it too. As a people who are obsessively concerned with good health, they are now equally fascinated with the concept of "staying young forever."

In October 1986, Sangyo Noritsu University in Tokyo published a book on this theme, *Springtime of Life*, by Sakuyama and Uno. It was an immediate sell-out and went into a second printing. By the end of 1987 it had gone into its 26th printing, one of the most popular best-sellers of all time. How many million copies of this book are now in print I cannot imagine, but I can imagine the impact it is having on the graying generation of Japan.

A young Japanese friend, knowing of this book I was writing on aging, sent me a copy in the original Japanese. Would that I could read it! But fortunately, the authors include some fine quotes in English.

MacArthur's high esteem in Japan is attested to by the photo of his memorial building in this book. With it is a section in English entitled "Youth," based on a poem by the late Samuel Ullman and presented to MacArthur.

Youth

"Youth is not a time of life — it is a state of mind; it is a quality of the imagination, a vigor of the emotions, a predominance of courage over timidity, of the appetitie for adventure over love of ease.

"Nobody grows old merely by living a number of years; people grow old only by deserting their ideals. *Years wrinkle the skin, but to give up enthusiasm wrinkles the soul.*

"Whether seventy or sixteen, there is in every being's heart the love of wonder, the sweet amazement at the stars and the starlike things and thoughts, the undaunted challenge of events, the unfailing childlike appetite for "what next," and the joy in the game of life.

"You are as young as your faith, as old as your doubt, as young as your self-confidence, as old as your fear, as young as your hope, as old as your despair.

"So long as your heart receives messages of beauty, cheer, courage, grandeur and power from the earth, from man and from the Infinite, so long you are young.

"When the wires are all down and the central place of your heart is covered with the snows of pessimism and the ice of cynicism, then you are grown old indeed, and may God have mercy on your soul."

Mid-Life Crisis

Many people feel that 50 is the watershed point between youth and old age. Once you've celebrated your 50th birthday, you're on the skids, on the downhill swoop to the end.

Nonsense, says Patrice Horn, of *Psychology Today*. You needn't have a mid-life crisis if you don't want one. It's largely in your attitude toward life as you approach middle age, she maintains. If you become obsessed with hot flashes and gray hairs and a bald head, of course you have a crisis. But it's not necessary.

I agree with Ms. Horn 100%. I know, because I missed that crisis completely. I was too deeply involved in founding a four-year international college to have time to think about my personal life. (See my book, *Miracle on a Mountain*, Strawberry Hill Press, 1987.)

I now discover, on counting up, that I was 51 when I was made president of that institution. Mid-life whim?

Indeed not. Getting the college going was the culmination of ten years of preparation and hard work. But the bottom line here is that I forgot myself completely — my age, my health, my life-long shyness — in the all-encompassing challenge of the task with which I was faced.

The Fountain of Age

The National Gallery of Art has developed a fascinating walking tour, with this title. The gripping idea behind this exhibit is that each of the pieces of art was created by an artist near the end of a long life. If you are ever fortunate enough to view this mind-boggling show, you will agree, "Grow old along with me; the best is yet to be."

One of the most spectacular pieces is John Miro's gigantic wool tapestry, some 36 by 15 feet. At age 70 Miro turned from painting to creating exciting textiles, and at 84 he designed and supervised the creation of this brilliant hanging, among others.

Titian was still painting when he was carried off by the plague in his 100th year. *Venus and Adonis*, the Titian on display here, probably the most sensuous and powerful of all his works, was painted when he was over 83.

Henri Matisse was immobilized by illness at 72, and by the time he was 79, he had to give up easel painting entirely. But that did not stop him. His most famous masterpieces were done by cutting with scissors patterns from brightly colored paper, all after he was 81. His lovely *Woman with Amphora and Pomegranates* was done in his 82nd year.

Some two dozen of the world's greatest artists are represented in this show, including Rembrandt, El Greco, Frans Hals, Degas, Cezanne, Corot, Turner, and Winslow Homer. It is a breath-taking display of the courage of age.

Say Yes to Life

Never say "no" to an exciting proposal. This has been my doctrine since the time I agreed to a friend's invitation to go to Nicaragua to teach during a three-month summer vacation. I was 40, with two little girls and a husband (who actually urged me to go). So the children and I flew south for an eventful summer in Managua.

Since then I have accepted intriguing invitations to teach two years in Japan, two seasons in Mexico, a year in Guayaquil, Ecuador, and one summer to conduct a lecture tour to London, Versailles, Vienna and Rome.

After retirement as dean of a girls' school, I earned a Master's Degree in playwriting and wrote more than a dozen plays, some published, some produced; I had published a historical novel, two books of nonfiction, and six books of poetry. Another half dozen books are seeking publication. No time to think about growing old!

It's in Your Attitude

"Achievement and creativity," says Douglas O. Woodruff, president of the American Association of Retired Persons (AARP), "know neither age nor time. And everyone deserves an opportunity to age successfully. It should be the norm, not the exception."

Now is the Time!

Join AARP (American Association of Retired Persons) today. You needn't be retired. For $5 anyone 50 years or over may join. It will be the best $5 you ever spent. In addition to a fine glossy bi-monthly magazine, *Modern Maturity*, you have available a wide range of services and information, ranging from prescription service and insurance to special travel rates and assistance with income tax. When you send your $5 enrollment check, ask for their booklet, *AARP—Its Programs, Its Services*. If you live east of the Mississippi, write to AARP, 1909 K. St. NW, Washington, DC 20049. If you live west of the Mississippi, write to AARP, P.O. Box 199, Long Beach, CA 90801.

Getting Older, Growing Younger, Barbara Cartland. Dodd, Mead and Co., New York, 1984. Your guide to living young, looking young and being beautiful inside and out. Ms. Cartland, step-grandmother of Princess Diana, is listed in *The Guinness Book of Records* as the world's top-selling writer. Champion of older people.

Gifts of Age, Charlotte Painter and Pamela Valois, Chronicle Books, San Francisco, 1985. Sensitive profiles of many women of advanced years who are still achieving and meeting the challenges of life.

Cowardice?
I only know we don't live twice,
Therefore — shun death, is my advice.
—Robert Browning

11. GREAT DOCTORS KILL MORE PEOPLE

I Didn't Say It!

The title of this chapter is quoted from the *Bulletin of the New York Academy of Medicine*, vol. V, 1929. The full quotation is, "I often say a great doctor kills more people than a great general," attributed to Baron von Leibnitz of the 17th century.

But I must say, it has a certain honest ring to it which has more than a little bearing on some of the things I am about to say. To attain the optimum level of health, I feel that we, the patients, as well as the medical profession, must make some radical changes.

How To Live To Be 100

Ever watch the *Today* show on NBC? I love Willard Scott and his amazing array of "Happy Birthday" photographs from across the country of people celebrating their one-hundredth birthdays.

But how many 100-year-olds will be celebrating birthdays in the year 2000, or in 2020? Not many, I'll wager, if we continue our mad pursuit of miracle drugs and record-shattering surgery. Don't misunderstand me. I don't deny the tremendous importance of medical research, both in drugs and in surgical procedures. I'm all for transplants, etc. *if* they make life better for the patient.

But would those centenarians have reached that golden age by transplants and miracle drugs? Or by running to the doctor with every sniffle or symptom? Or by spending hours in a doctor's office for numerous check-ups and tests? I'll bet a dollar for every birthday candle that they rarely rely on a doctor for anything.

Old Family Doctors

In Grandma's day, doctors were totally dedicated to the well-being of their patients. They brought us into the world in the family bedroom, and watched us depart in the same place. No sterile, heartless hospital rooms. I don't recommend a return to that archaic time, but I like the fact that the family doctor knew us intimately, and cared for us from birth to death. He knew the entire family and what made it tick. He "cared" for us, in the deepest meaning of that word.

They Didn't See Us Often

Year after year would go by when we never saw a doctor. We didn't know what a dentist was. Mom was fanatical about our brushing our teeth regularly with salt and baking soda. We never went to bed without lining up out in the backyard for the family "scrubdown," weather permitting. In winter, we took turns over the kitchen slop bucket, scrubbing our teeth until they gleamed. No one in the family ever had a cavity or a toothache, partly, I suspect, because we seldom had anything with sugar in it. And at 79, my teeth are still excellent.

We stayed well because of the way we lived. We ate

only natural simple foods. There was no other kind. Our food was not "processed" in any way, except for what we did to it ourselves there on the ranch. We helped Mom can (in glass jars) peas, beans, pickled beets, tomatoes and fruit. Dad butchered our own pigs and smoked the hams and bacons; the pigs, incidentally, had been fed nothing but natural food themselves. The only food processed off the ranch was our flour. Dad would haul several sacks of our wheat to the flour mill 20 miles away, leaving at dawn and returning late at night with sacks of white flour (not really "white," but a rich cream color, for it was not bleached), some whole wheat flour (graham flour, we called it) and cracked wheat cereal. We did buy oatmeal, which Dad insisted we eat almost daily; the mill wasn't equipped to roll our oats, which we fed to the horses, or sold. We were a healthy lot, horses and all.

No Morning Sit-Ups

There were early morning "get-ups" instead. Dad was always the first one up. As soon as he got a good fire blazing in the kitchen stove, he roused the rest of us out without ceremony, for he had no patience with "lazy bones." From then on it was busy, busy, busy until time to go to bed. Everything was *hard* work.

Why All This Nostalgia?

I wouldn't return to those days for a million-dollar jackpot. But the point is that the people whose 100th birthdays Willard Scott celebrates lived that kind of life.

My point? Eat right and exercise vigorously, and you won't *need* doctors often. You may reach 100, too!

Self-Help

Today the medical profession scoffs at "self help." "Folk medicine!" they snort in disgust. "Sheer drivel! And dangerous besides."

Many doctors today tend to lump vitamins along with "folk medicine and other quackery." Even beloved Senator Claude Pepper, who was the nation's most powerful advocate for the senior population, scoffed at vitamin therapy. He even attempted to outlaw the sale of vitamins without a doctor's prescription. (He certainly heard from me on that one.) His rather lame response was that he just wanted to save the old people from wasting their money. Baloney! They have been using their own common sense and money for a lifetime!

Why Doctors Fear Vitamins

Senator Pepper allowed doctors to sway his judgment. Many doctors harbor an innate fear that their patients, if they keep themselves well through "folk medicine, vitamins and other quackery," will eliminate a hefty portion of the doctors' incomes.

Do they *say* that is the reason? Good heavens, no! They *say* that if the public is allowed to take their own health into their own hands, they will be subjecting themselves to"dangerous side effects." Razz-berries! As a solid gold experimental guinea pig of the medical profession for the past 35 years, I have suffered innumerable severe and sometimes life-threatening side effects caused by an endless array of drugs to which they have subjected me. Some day I plan to write a book on that topic. A long book.

All that doctors really fear is the loss of income and prestige.

Attitudes Must Change

It's not all the doctors' fault. It's what they're taught in medical schools. Most doctors are great people. Sincere. Dedicated. Idealistic. I've known many, in my years of living around the world. But two faults lie within the med schools.

First, most doctors are taught little about nutrition and vitamin supplements. The nutrition courses they get in most schools are sketchy at best. And doctors fear what they know nothing about.

Second, most physicians are trained both by medical schools and by the public, to believe that they are omnipotent. By the time they graduate, serve their internship, and become licensed, they are looked upon as infallible and all-wise, a kind of professional "god" to the "uninformed public." Even a simple question often arouses anger. They feel that their authority is being challenged. Even though all you want to know is a way to stay healthier, they resent it.

"What do you think of vitamin C?" I asked my doctor. "Adelle Davis says it strengthens the immune system."

"Don't ever mention that woman's name in this office again!" he exploded. "She has caused me more trouble than all the rest of my practice put together!"

And he was not unique. Almost every doctor I have encountered has responded in the same way. "Nothing but quackery!"

A Lot Is Our Own Fault

Too long have we destroyed our own health by ignorance and sheer willful negligence. We drink alcohol to excess. We smoke. We make love promiscuously. We use drugs, both legal and illegal. We eat to excess. We eat foods that are destructive to health. We have become too fat and lazy to walk to the neighborhood grocery store. It's easier and quicker to get in the car and drive. We devour tons of "fast foods," loaded with the three deadly sins — salt, sugar, and fats. We drive ourselves into an early grave through an obstinate "who cares?" attitude.

Then, dying of any number of illnesses brought on by our own carelessness —against doctor's orders — we appear at his office, demanding, "Fix me! Make me well! Fast, because I'm in a hurry!" And if he doesn't, or can't, we are extremely annoyed.

Two Choices

When faced by a frantic patient, the doctor usually has two choices. Surgery. Or miracle drugs.

Personally, I am convinced that any invasion of the body, either by surgical methods or by drugs, is something to avoid if at all possible. If the treatment does not improve the quality of life, why have it? No artificial hearts for me, thanks! I plan to die with my boots on, as my grandparents did before me, and their grandparents before them. No heroic endeavors to sustain a meaningless life, please.

Second Opinion

Just today I heard Dr. Art Uline speaking about carotid surgery to clear the blood vessel leading to the brain. He said that in one-third of the patients the results were disastrous, in another third there was no improvement, and in only a third was there the slightest improvement.

"Get a second opinion!" urges Dr. Uline. "Most of those patients should never have had the surgery. Considering such a hazardous operation, one should get the opinion of a second doctor, and not one who will be connected to the surgery or will benefit from it in any way."

I have benefitted from a second opinion on four different occasions. The second doctor said, "No surgery!" in every case.

Let's Become Partners

Let's make some changes in the attitudes taught in medical schools. Doctors should be trained in "wellness." Now they are being trained only for "illness." A doctor would rather be faced with a really ill patient, one that fits a case history of some disease studies in med school, than to answer the questions of a person who prefers to stay well.

My vision of a medical Utopia would be one in which people and their doctors are full partners in maintaining health to the optimum degree. Where advice on *staying* healthy is shared. And where doctors consider themselves *partners* in medical decisions — but not God, making unilateral decisions on hospitalization, surgery and drugs. Let them treat the patient as an intelligent, well-read partner, and not a bag of cement to be shifted around at their own convenience, without thought of his desires, questions or needs.

Our Greatest Treasure

The most valuable thing we possess, and actually, the

only thing that is truly ours, is our own body. What a miraculously complicated and beautiful machine it is! Now let's keep it that way. Let's not wreck it, and then haul it in to the repair shop, hoping to get a new motor slipped in under the hood.

Take Cancer

The word sends shocks of terror into our hearts. We used to think of it as an "old people's disease." No more. Even baby girls die of uterine cancer. And ten-year-old boys have to have cancerous legs amputated.

Melanoma, a most deadly form of skin cancer, is on the rise. And so is the national passion for sun-tanned skin.

Last year at "spring break" I watched on TV the annual orgy of sun madness, as nearly nude students packed the beaches of Florida and Southern California.

"Don't you worry about skin cancer?" asked a roving reporter.

"No," laughed the students carelessly. "By the time we get it, they'll have figured out a cure for it."

There you are. Leave it to the doctor to fix.

Fats and Cancer

Research repeatedly tells us that colon and rectal cancers are largely the product of high fat intake. And now they have discovered that breast cancer in women also thrives on fat in the diet. But will these important discoveries, and the succeeding warnings, cut down the crowded lines to fast food outlets, where a large part of the nation's fat is consumed? I'll bet not. "If I get cancer, let the doctor fix it."

94

Thank You for Not Smoking

I put this neat little sign near my front door shortly after my husband's death from lung cancer. He had always smoked. My friends respect that sign, for they know, and they also know of my own violently asthmatic reaction to tobacco.

But who should come to my door with a cigarette in his hand but my grandson, who had been with his beloved grandfather in the hospital the night he died. I could scarcely believe my eyes. The young think they are indestructible.

Open Wide and Say No

Are frequent dental x-rays and check-ups necessary? I have a remarkable dentist who says no. If you have good teeth, don't meddle with them, is his theory. No long ago I made an appointment with him.

"What can I do for you today?" he asked as I settled into the dental chair. "Anything wrong?"

"No, but it's been two years. I thought maybe I should have my teeth cleaned."

He looked them over carefully.

"They don't need cleaning. They're perfect. I can see that you clean and floss them regularly. No plaque. And I can tell that you don't drink carbonated drinks. Worst thing in the world for teeth. And you have a good balanced diet. No sign of decay. And your gums are pink and healthy."

I laughed as he finished.

"I'm just remembering the last dentist I had. He was angry if I didn't come in every six months for dental x-rays and a tooth scaling."

"I don't think much of x-rays," he answered honestly. "Unless I feel there's a real problem. Too dangerous. Causes lots of cancer, in my judgment. And most scaling is injurious to the enamel and the tender gum tissues if we aren't cautious. No need for scaling if you care for your teeth properly. I advise patients who are troubled with plaque to brush with Colgate or Crest. Both of them have anti-plaque formula."

Thank God for a dentist with ethics!

But occasional dental check-ups are valuable, especially if you have inflamed or bleeding gums. Gingivitis, a bacterial gum infection common to some 40% of the population, is painless and can, if not treated, develop into periodontal disease, which can cost you a whole mouth full of perfectly healthy teeth. Just ask your dentist to skip the regular x-rays. If he refuses, get another dentist. I did.

Everyone Has Cancer

That is the startling theory that one of my medical friends believes. Dr. Smith says, "Everyone has cancer, if he lives long enough. After all, we must all die of something as we approach our final days. And cancer is one of the most common diseases.

"We all have cancer past middle age. If the body is not traumatized in some way, the cancer lies there, almost dormant, growing *very* slowly. But if the body is injured, either by surgery or other physical or emotional truma, those sleeping cancer cells go wild.

"That's why we often find breast cancer occurs, or is discovered, following a severe emotional trauma, such as the death of a spouse or child or parent, or after a divorce or a painful change of career, or home. That is even true with pets. Dogs and cats often die of leukemia shortly after the loss of an owner, or after changing homes.

"The important thing to remember is that cancer develops more slowly, the older we get. So even if a person is full of cancer in old age, if surgery or other trauma does not disturb the body balance, that person will probably die of something else before the cancer is discovered."

I'm counting on it, Doc! At 79, I plan to let my "mushrooms" grow slowly and silently, without any more surgery to upset my busy life. I'm living at an amazingly exciting clip now, but if I had surgery, regardless of how "successful" it might be, my life would be demolished. I prefer to die naturally, "when my time has come," as they used to say.

Mystery?

A strange phenomenon occurred in California not long ago when the state's doctors went out on strike. The death rate suddenly dropped to an amazingly low level. Why? Could it be because the operating rooms were closed? Let's take charge of our own health. Let's not turn the entire burden of our health over to the doctors and the operating rooms.

People's Medical Society

Spend $15 for a year's membership in this organization, an outgrowth of *Prevention*. It will be the best $15 you ever invested, for it's a fearless, straight forward, pull-no-punches look at the medical profession from the standpoint of the consumer. Let me quote from its president, Charles B. Inlander, in setting forth his aims:

"*First* — to help right the wrongs in our medical and health-care systems that rob so many Americans of their health and money.

"*Second* — to promote interest in reliable self-care...to provide you with the sound information needed for that care...and to direct you to other sources of such information and help, so that you and others may become more aware health consumers and make more enlightened decisions about your health.

"By doing these things, we are helping you (and others) get back what is rightfully yours —control over the health-care system that affects your life so deeply." (People's Medical Society, 14 E. Minor St., Emmaus, PA 18049)

Use Your Head

Be conscious of that marvelous body you have. You'll never have another. Cherish it. Do all the *right* things! Stay well on your own, as long as is humanly possible. Barring hazards of the environment (which we'd better do something about, incidentally) or some congenital disease, you have at *least* 100 years of youthful living coming to you. Use it! Enjoy it!

Bonne santé!

Some great reading (to help you participate in your own health):

Type 1/Type 2 Allergy Relief, Alan Scott Levin, M.D. and Merla Zellerbach, Houghton Mifflin, New York, 1983.
The Allergy Self-Help Book, Sharon Faelton and Editors of *Prevention*, Rodale Press, Emmaus, PA, 1983

The Arthritic's Cookbook, Collin H. Don, M.D. and Jane
  Banks, Crowell, New York, 1973
Anatomy of an Illness as Perceived by the Patient, Norman
  Cousins, Norton, 1979
Better Homes and Gardens Family Medical Guide, Donald
  G. Cooley, Editor, Meredith Corp. 1973. A complete
  encyclopedia of health and the human body.
Chelation Therapy, Dr. Morton Walker, '76 Press, Atlanta,
  1980. How to prevent or reverse hardening of the
  arteries.
Cold Comfort, Hal Zina Bennett, Clarkson N. Potter, Inc.,
  New York, 1979. Colds and flu: everybody's guide to
  self treatment.
Complete Guide to Prescription and Non-Prescription Drugs,
  H. Winter Griffith, M.D., HP Books, 1983
Dr. Atkins' Nutrition Breakthrough, Robert C. Atkins, M.D.,
  Morrow and Co., New York, 1981. How to treat your
  medical conditions without drugs.
Encyclopedia of Common Diseases, J.I. Rodale and staff,
  Rodale Press, 1974
Encyclopedia of Natural Home Remedies, Mark Bricklin,
  Rodale Press, Emmaus, PA, 1982
The Family Physician for Home Use, Dr. Herman Pomeranz
  and Dr. Irvin S. Koll, Greystone Press, 1951
How To Be Your Own Doctor Sometimes, Keith W. Sehnert,
  M.D. with Howard Eisenberg, Grosset and Dunlap,
  New York, 1975.
How To Fight Ten Common Diseases, Editors, Rodale Press,
  Emmaus, PA, 1986. Valuable insights on hypertension,
  pneumonia, skin cancer, gallstones, diverticulitis,
  hemorrhoids, cataracts, osteoarthritis, artherosclerosis
  and osteoporosis.
Killing Cancer, The Jason Winters Story, Jason Winters, M
  and R Pubishing, Las Vegas, NV, 1980
Love, Medicine and Miracles, Bernie S. Siegal, M.D., Harper
  and Row, 1986. Lesson learned about self-healing from
  a surgeon's experience with patients who have the

courage to work with their doctors to participate in their own recovery.

Medicine on Trial, Charles Inlander, Lowell Levin and Ed Weiner, Prentice Hall, New York, 1988. The appalling story of ineptitude, malfeasance, neglect and arrogance in the field of medicine by those we trust.

The Medicine Show, Editors of *Consumer Reports*, Consumers Union, Mt. Vernon, New York, 1971. Some plain truths about popular products for common ailments; medical supplies worth buying; choosing a family doctor.

Natural Home Remedies, Mark Bricklin, Rodale Press, Emmaus, PA, 1982

Natural Healing Annual 1986, Mark Bricklin, Rodale Press, 1986

Natural Self-Care, Editors of *Prevention*, Rodale Press, 1988. Tips on feeling and looking good, healing yourself naturally, and easing pain the natural way.

Physicians' Desk Reference for Prescription Drugs, Charles Baker, Editor, Medical Economics Co., Oradell, NJ, 1975

Physicians' Desk Reference for Non-Prescription Drugs, Charles E. Baker, Medical Economics Co., 1980. For the the current edition of both the above, write: Physicians' Desk Reference, Box 58, Oradell, NJ 07649

Prescription Drug Encyclopedia, Gayle Cawood, M.Ed., F.C. and A. Inc., Peachtree City, GA, 1987

Prescription Drugs, Peggy Boucher Muller, Pharm.C. Crown Publishers, 1983

Prescription Drugs: Effects and Side Effects, Edward L. Stern, Grosset and Dunlap, New York, 1975

Prevention Mailbag of Natural Remedies, Mark Bricklin, Rodale Press, 1984

Preventive Medicine: Membership Directory. International Academy of Nutrition and Preventive Medicine, Box 5832, Lincoln, NE 68505. (402)476-2716

Psycho-Nutrition, Carlton Fredericks, Ph.D., Grosset and Dunlap, New York, 1976. Vital role of diet and vitamin therapy in preventing and curing mental illness.

The Realms of Healing, Stanley Krippner and Alberto
Villoldo, Celestial Arts, Millbrae, CA, 1976. Scientific
laboratory research in paranormal healing in Canada,
USSR, Brazil and USA.

Rights for the Critically Ill, John A. Robertson, Bantam
Books, New York, 1983. An American Civil Liberties
Handbook.

Second Opinion, Isadore Rosenfeld, M.D., Bantam Books,
New York, 1982. This indispensable book may help
you avoid unnecessary surgery.

Self-Healing: My Life and Vision, Meir Schneider, Routledge
and Kegan Paul, New York, 1987. Through exercise
and other techniques, the author cured himself of
congenital blindness, and now teaches thousands of
others, some with "incurable" diseases, to heal
themselves.

Self-Help Manual for Arthritis Patients, Judith L. Klinger,
Arthritis Foundation, 3400 Peachtree Rd. N.E., Atlanta,
GA 30326

Take This Book to the Hospital With You, Charles B.
Inlander and Ed Weiner, Rodale Press, Emmaus, PA,
1985. A consumer guide to surviving your hospital stay.

A Taste of My Own Medicine, Dr. Edward Rosenbaum,
Random House, New York, 1988. When doctor is
patient. "This is a courageous book..." -Norman Cousins

Worst Pills, Best Pills, Sidney M. Wolfe, M.D., Public Citizens
Health Research Group, Washington DC, 1988. The
older adult's guide to avoiding drug-induced death or
illness. Write to Public Citizens Health Research Group,
2000 P St. NW, Suite 700, Washington, DC 20036

*Your Prescription and You: A Pharmacy Handbook for
Consumers*, Steven Strauss, Ph.D., R.Ph., Medical
Business Services, 1977

The Challenge of Age, E. Fritz Schmerl, M.D. and Sally
Patterson Tubach, Continuum, New York, 1986. In
this comprehensive, lively book a noted geriatrician

dispels the myth that old age must be equated with disease and depression.

The Pulse Test: The Secret of Building Your Basic Health, Arthur F. Coca, M.D., Lyle Stuart, Inc., Secaucus, NJ, 1982. Allergies can cause high blood pressure, diabetes, ulcers, epilepsy, migraine, constipation, "that tired feeling," spells of dizziness, backaches and mental depression. By the pulse test, you can find out if food allergies are causing your illness.

Drug Worksheet for Patient, Family, Doctor, and Pharmacist. May be obtained by sending $1.50 to Public Citizen Health Research Group, Dept. DW, 2000 P St. NW, Washington, DC 20036. Can be extremely helpful in avoiding illness or death by interaction of drugs and prescriptions.

Cantrol: Dietary Guidelines and Program Overview. Remarkable treatment for eradicating *Candida albicans* (gastointestinal yeast infection), commonly misunderstood and misdiagnosed by physicians. Available in health food stores, or write: Nature's Way Products, Inc., 10 Mountain Springs Parkway, Springville, UT 84663

Linus Pauling Institute of Science and Medicine, 440 Page Mill Road, Palo Alto, CA 94306. For a modest donation to the magnificent research being conducted by Nobel-winner Pauling and his Institute in the fields of cancer and other health concerns, you will receive his valuable *Newsletter*, reporting on recent health discoveries.

People's Medical Society, 14 East Minor St., Emmaus, PA 18049. For $15 you can become a member, entitling you to a wide array of items from their health library at a reduced price. Splendid watchdog organization protecting consumers from failures of the medical profession. Highly recommended.

Prevention Magazine, 33 East Minor St., Emmaus, PA 18098. Top ranking monthly, giving the latest knowledge available in the field of preventive medicine.

He loved his youth, and his youth has become eternal.
—Lord Tweedsmuir

12. THE VITAMIN WAY TO YOUTH

Why Are We Vitamin Deficient?

Why are the elderly usually vitamin deficient, while young people and children are not? Why do we need to take supplements, while our children and grandchildren are full of vim and vinegar without them? What's the difference?

One reason is that with decreased activity and a lower basal metabolic rate, we don't need as many calories. Yet our need for vitamins, minerals and protein remains the same as when we were 20.

"That means we have to be highly selective, and pretty darned smart, to pack the same nutrients into a smaller calorie quota," says Dr. Paul Lachance of Rutger's Cook College.

"And in addition, by the time we're 70, we're down to about 35% of the functioning taste buds we had at 30. This is one of the reasons older people lose interest in food." And the reason so many elderly eat more sweets, which in turn decreases their appetite for wholesome foods. (Taste buds, however, can be rejuvenated by zinc and vitamin A supplements, as can the sense of smell, which in turn enhances the sense of taste.)

Digestive efficiency begins to decline with the passing years, as we secrete less enzymes and stomach acid.

For this reason we absorb less iron and vitamin B, as well as calcium and minerals, necessitating a greater intake.

Medications interfere with vitamin and mineral usage also. Diuretics for high blood pressure and weight loss flush potassium from our bodies, so this must be replaced if we remain healthy. Zinc and magnesium are other life necessities that are lost through medication.

Loss of teeth is another problem in eating a normal diet. By age 70, Dr. Lachance says, 28% of the men and 38% of the women have lost all their teeth, and only 20% have been replaced by satisfactory dentures. Therefore a large portion of the elderly population must be satisfied with food they can cope with, regardless of its nutritional value, such as applesauce and noodles.

DNA, the Miraculous Blueprint

Yet another reason for our increased need for vitamins as we grow older is the fact that we all come equipped at birth with a wonderful little book of instructions, a blueprint, really, of how each individual organ in each individual person is programmed to react in a certain way. No two individuals are exactly the same. This pattern-substance or "software" is called DNA (deoxyribonucleic acid). But with years of use, the pattern tends to become a bit blurred and sometimes fails to send out its code symbols properly, so that the body's cells fail to duplicate themselves.

Scientists believe that this failure is due to the action of "free radicals," fragments of a molecule that have been torn from their source, and are wildly trying to tie on to another molecule. When they succeed, they injure and sometimes destroy their host. Free radicals are produced by oxidation in the bloodstream (as happens in suntanning, in the stresses and strains of aging, and in exposure to certain chemicals).

My Guru

Any man who is smart enough to earn two unshared Nobel Prizes (the only person in the world to have done so) is smart enough for me. And the man who can discover a cure for the common cold is No. 1 in my book. Linus Pauling. Why shouldn't I listen to such a man?

I was not too well-read in science and had been living outside the U.S., so I didn't remember who Linus Pauling was until his book, *Vitamin C and the Common Cold*, came out in 1970. I'd been taking vitamin C regularly for some years, but hadn't found it could really kill a cold. I had many fewer colds than before, but "C" didn't really stop a cold.

Then I read the book. Dr. Pauling was recommending "megadoses," not the one-a-day routine I'd been following.

He suggested increasing the doseage until we find it truly effective, ten to twenty grams.

"There is no danger involved," he said. "I take 10 grams a day just to maintain the optimum in good health. The only side effect is a diarrhea when one has reached the maximum dosage necessary to fight the infection. Each person is different and requires a different level of the vitamin. There is no such thing as over-dosing, since any surplus is flushed out by the kidneys, with the onset of a diarrhea indicating the saturation point. The diarrhea stops as soon as the dosage is reduced."

Ten grams! That is 10,000 milligrams, just 100 times the dose I had been taking! I dared to follow Pauling's advice. Upping the dosage was the secret to success. I find now that I can control a cold — stamp it out — if I take it in doses high enough, and catch it in time. Vitamin C also controls hay fever and associated allergy symptoms, I am delighted to report.

Personally, I am eternally grateful to Dr. Pauling for eradicating those miserable winters of sore throats and sinus infections, and those horrid summers of hay fever and sneezing. I gladly send a donation every month to the Linus Pauling Institute of Science and Medicine in Palo Alto, to help them with their research in cancer and other diseases. If he has stopped the common cold, he can do anything!

For those who say, "I've tried C and it doesn't do a thing for me," I respond, "Your C was either too little or too late."

I know whereof I speak. For almost 20 years I've read everything available on the subject, and have done intensive research (personal trial and error). Now, during the cold season and during the high pollen season, I take at least a gram at each meal and at bedtime, 4,000 milligrams daily. If I have a flare-up of coughing, sneezing, or sore throat, I up my intake to as much as six grams every time the symptom occurs. The only side effect is frequent urination — much preferable to being sick a week with a cold!

Another Nutrition Nut

Garson Kanin, one of America's favorite directors and playwrights, recently celebrated his 75th birthday. Still trim and bursting with vitality, he is one of the leaders and movers in the theatre world. He was the man responsible for *The Diary of Ann Frank*, *Funny Girl*, and *Born Yesterday*, among a long list of hits.

He is also the author of many books, including *Tracy and Hepburn*, *Remembering Mr. Maugham*, and *It Takes a Long Time to Become Young*. In the latter, he admits that he is a "nutrition nut" and proud of it. He lives on megadoses of vitamins of a wide assortment. But vitamin C is the one he swears by, ten grams (10,000 milligrams) daily.

Ruth Gordon, his wife of many years, shared his interest in health and nutrition. Although a generation older than Garson, Ruth remained active in the theatre until her death recently. This lively and fascinating couple have been a marvel to the theatre world for decades. It was Ruth's leading role in *Harold and Maude* where she shone as what she was, a splendid actress.

The Kanin apartment is next door to Katharine Hepburn's, another amazing actress who has been starring in films since 1932. What is the secret of these three?

"Health has everything to do with it," says Kanin. "Youth is really being well, not a chronological age. A guy of 22 with ulcers and sclerosis of the liver is old, no matter what his age is." For Kanin, vitamins mean health.

Discovery of Gold in America

Barbara Cartland, Britain's beloved beauty and romance writer, first came to America in 1948, on a business trip with her husband.

"It was a total loss," she says in her book, *I Searched for Rainbows*, "except for one significant thing: I discovered vitamins!"

"There is a most wonderful new thing here," someone in New York told her. "Americans have found that they can drink as much as they like and if they take some of these capsules the next day, they don't have a hangover!"

Mrs. Cartland was not a drinker but this mystery potion intrigued her.

"What is it?" she asked.

"Something they call vitamin B."

She bought some. The results were marvelous. She felt so well she bought some to take home to her children. Then she realized that it was a vitamin B deficiency that was affecting all Britons, brought on by wrong foods, anxiety, worry, and the nervous strain of WWII. That was when she began her drive for vitamins for Britain, which was to touch all English people in the years to come, as well as people around the world.

When she was on the verge of death after surgery in 1952, she ordered a different doctor (not the one who had operated) to give her some vitamins intravenously. After the injection, her recovery was sudden and miraculous. Then she went to the local breweries and collected huge tubs of brewer's yeast for the pigs she raised on her estate. That first season, her sows produced an average of 12 healthy piglets apiece, unheard of in England. She was off on her drive for vitamins for animals as well as people.

Sex and Vitamins

How many couples have gotten a divorce, Cartland reasoned, because what they thought was incompatibility was really a vitamin deficiency? So in 1959 she wrote a book, *Vitamins and Vitality*, to prove that the vitamins that make a man and women feel healthy can also make them passionate and responsive.

Then Barbara Cartland launched the National Association for Health, ringing in all the lords and ladies and marchionesses and dukes and duchesses and counts and earls she could capture, for a launching party at the Savoy. These people helped her promote health stores all over the country. Cartland became the president of the new organization, swept along by the enthusiasm of her friends, as well as by other admirers throughout Britain.

Vitamins were in for the Brits!

She'll Never Walk Again

"I think you'd better come, Auntie 'Cile," phoned my niece from Denver. "Mom is in the hospital, paralyzed from the waist down. They say she'll never walk again."

Vernice had suffered with multiple sclerosis for years, but this sudden turn for the worse frightened us all, even her doctors. I caught the first flight to Denver.

"Are you taking vitamins?" was my first question, after I kissed her dear beautiful face propped up on a hospital pillow.

She just shook her head. She didn't have much confidence in my "kinky" ideas.

"Would you take them if I bought you some?"

She shook her head again. "The doctor wouldn't let me if you did."

I was not discouraged. I sat by her bed day after day, and when her young doctor finally came in, I nabbed him with my proposal.

"If I buy them, would you let her take some vitamins?"

"Well..." he hedged uneasily. "I'd have to see exactly what you plan to give her first."

"Here's the list of what I take every day." I was ready with the list, and the size of doses. Curiously he looked into my healthy countenance. "I'm her older sister," I added.

One by one, he went down the list, okaying each vitamin as he went. "I can't see how they can do her any damage," he said a bit skeptically.

I rushed off to the nearest health food store and bought over $100 worth of nutrients. I swear, I could see the sudden improvement in her the next morning. By the end of the week, she had recovered feeling in her feet, and could even move her toes. Each day the improvement was dramatic.

The next time I visited Denver, she was home and walking about the house. She had many more happy years at home. I'll always believe that those vitamins had some bearing on her remarkable remission.

The ABCs of Youth

Here they are, the vitamins and minerals that you need to remain as young as possible as long as possible. I give credit to Robert M. Giller, M.D., and his priceless book, *Medical Makeover* (Morrow, 1986), as well as to *Prevention Magazine* and the invaluable information they have given me for the past 15 years. I must add, however, that everything I recommend here I have proven to be of the greatest efficacy in maintaining my own buoyant good health and verve for living. The daily doses here are recommended by Dr. Giller.

Vitamin A helps maintain normal health of the body tissues, especially of the mucous membranes, as in the nose, throat, and lungs. It is helpful in fighting colds and allergies, and in warding off the ravages of air pollution. It is especially important in maintaining healthy eyes. As it is fat-soluble, it can build up in the body, so care must be taken *not* to overdose, for the effects can be toxic.

Daily Dosage: 10,000 to 25,000 IU

Vitamin B12 is essential for the metabolism of all foods. It is needed for the building of red blood cells and for healthy nerves.

According to Dr. Paul Lachance of Cook College, Rutger's, common and amazingly prevalent senility can be quickly cured by proper intake of vitamin B. Too many people do not get nearly adequate levels of the vitamin to maintain mental and physical health. Supplements are therefore a necessity.

Even a slight deficiency of vitamin B12, says Dr. Lachance, can cause fatigue, irritability, and numbness. More severe deficiencies duplicate the symptoms of Alzheimer's. So to be sure, try the B route first.

Daily Dosage: 1000 to 3000 mcg. (micrograms)

Pantothenic Acid, another of the B complex, helps the body digest food and utilize vitamins. It helps resist stress and has been proven to prevent wrinkles and aging to a certain extent. Pantothenic acid is also recommended for recurring colds and sore throat, as well as ulcerative colitis.

Daily Dosage: 50 to 1000 mg.

B Complex. One of B's most treasured qualities for me personally is its wonderful ability to clear up canker sores, a malady I've had since early childhood. A couple of B-100s can stop the pain within minutes. Continue this double dosage until the lesion heals. Otherwise use the regular doses.

Daily Dosage: one B-100 three times daily

Vitamin C is the one supplement I cannot live without. Some believers call it "the Fountain of Youth." I call it "the Savior of Mankind." If I were to be left on a desert island with but one companion, it would be a barrel of vitamin C. It strengthens the immune system; clears up asthma, colds, hay fever; protects against air pollutants; cures gingivitis (gum disease); clears up bruise marks; helps keep down cholesterol; protects against a recurrence of heart attacks; and by building up the immune system, protects against cancer and other disease.

Humans are the only animals that can't produce their own supply of vitamin C. It is available in citrus fruits, potatoes, tomatoes, strawberries, and dark green vegetables, but the average person cannot possibly eat enough to get sufficient vitamin C to stay at the optimum of good health.

Dr. Linus Pauling and Ewan Cameron, M.D., have worked together for many years, proving the use of vitamin C in cancer treatment. In countless cases they have used it to alleviate cancer pain and to eventually put the cancer into complete remission. Much of this exciting and successful work is recorded in their book, *Cancer and Vitamin C* (W.W. Norton and Co., 1979). American doctors, still skeptical, fight vigorously against vitamin C therapy.

Stress depletes vitamin C, hence the increased need of this essential vitamin in today's society. Years before I had ever heard of vitamin C, I noted that a cold invariably followed on the heels of an emotional blow-up for any member of my family. Now I understand why.

Warning: Don't cease taking megadoses of vitamin C suddenly. Such cessation may bring on a backlash resembling scurvy. Ease off gradually. Don't take large doses if you have a tendency to kidney stones. The only side effects of vitamin C are frequent urination and bowel movements, which immediately clear up with reduction of doseage. No known toxicity.

Daily Dosage: 1000 mg. to infinity, as needed

Vitamin D is sunshine in a capsule. If you are out in the sunlight most of the day, it is probable you don't need this supplement. But don't forget the dangers of too much sun — Catch-22 situation. So it's much safer to take a cod-liver oil capsule daily to help utilize and absorb the calcium you need in your teeth and bones, and to maintain a healthy heart and nervous system, especially if you live in northern climes where the winters are long and cloudy. Vitamin D can be toxic in overdoses, so be careful.

Daily Dosage: 400 IU

Vitamin E is the only vitamin that is known to work both internally and externally. Taken internally it acts as an antioxidant, protecting us from the free radicals which cause cancer, blood clots, and premature aging. Vitamin E keeps the blood vessels supple. Externally applied, it clears up cold sores, and is recommended by some specialists as a wrinkle retardant when applied in the form of cream to the face.

Warning: Be cautious with vitamin E if you have high blood pressure, suffer from excessive bleeding from wounds, or are taking birth control pills.

Daily Dosage: 400 to 800 IU

Minerals are Essential, Too

Calcium is a necessity for all humans — for teeth and bones, for energy production, for blood clotting, for healthy muscles and nerves, for regulation of heart beat, and for maintaining immunity against disease.

But as we grow older, it is of crucial importance when osteroporosis attacks us, withering the elderly into mere shadows of our youthful selves. Although men suffer from this condition also, it is among women after menopause that it becomes a real threat to life, as their bones become thin and brittle. A little tumble and a broken hip can send us to the hospital (and often to an early grave).

The elimination of dairy products in the diet (because of milk allergies and low-cholesterol diets) is one cause of insufficient calcium in the system. Another is because we utilize only 20-30% of the calcium we get from tablets. One reason for this is that we don't absorb calcium if taken with food, says Dr. Giller in *Medical Makeover*. He recommends taking the calcium in liquid form at bedtime.

I think I have proven that I am getting ample calcium,

despite no milk products, by the fact that I have never broken a bone in any of my many serious falls, requiring numerous stitches. X = crossed fingers!

One final rule: calcium must be combined with exercise to be truly effective in preventing bone loss.

Daily Dosage: 1000-3000 mg.

Magnesium is an essential for all life. We could not utilize any of our food or minerals without it. Although it is found in whole grains, nuts and raw green leafy vegetables, it is impossible to get enough for optimum health without supplements. Since it is essential in assimilation of calcium, I recommend (and practice) taking the two together in the form of dolomite, nature's own combination.

Dolomite is a marvelous relaxer and soother of minor aches and pains.

Daily Dosage: 3 tablets upon retiring

Chromium is a very tiny but essential part of our body's needs. It is the element that controls the enzymes which convert sugar to energy. It also controls synthesis of fats, proteins, and cholesterol. It is of life-saving importance especially to people with blood-sugar problems, diabetics and hypoglycemics, for it balances the sugar content of the blood. As a hypoglycemic, I find it marvelous in controlling the "after-dinner droop," the overpowering weariness and sleepiness that follows a meal containing carbohydrates.

Daily Dosage: 200 to 600 mcg.

Selenium has been found to be of great value in protecting us from cancer, frequent sore throats, angina, heart disease, air pollution, and hazards of a high-fat diet. It is of utmost importance as an antioxidant, thus prolonging youth. (Caution: don't overdose, as it can be lethal.)

Daily Dosage: 50 to 200 mcg.

Zinc is a mineral of such far-reaching uses that it should be taken with each meal. It enhances the sense of smell and taste, a great boon to elders who have lost it. It protects us against colds, gastric ulcers, prostate problems, the carbohydrate imbalance of diabetes and hypoglycemia, acne, boils, body odor, and both osteoarthritis and rheumatoid arthritis. It helps increase sex drive and sperm count (in case you're interested).

Daily Dosage: 50 mg. (4 times daily) = 200 mg.

Copper is necessary in formation of red blood cells, in healthy function of the nerves, and in activity of enzymes. It works with vitamin C to maintain the elasticity of the blood vessels, lungs and skin. It is shown to be of value in protection against cancer and heart disease, and to relieve the pain of arthritis.

Since copper and zinc complement each other, it is important that you get both.

Daily Dosage: 2 mg.

Iron is of utmost importance to menstruating women, but to the rest of us as well, especially if we have cut down on intake of red meat to eliminate fats (iron is found largely in beef). It is important to anyone losing blood, through hiatal hernia, hemorrhoids, peptic ulcers, colitis, diverticulitis, or to anyone with anemia.

Iron is best utilized if taken between meals, and not with food.

Daily Dosage: 60 to 120 mg.

Iodine is of special importance to those of us who have cut down on salt intake. Iodized salt used to insure us against thyroid malfunction. Now most of us who eat a lot of seafood are still protected, but since iodine is crucial to our hearts and immune system, we must make sure.

We can do this by taking one or two kelp tablets daily, or by being sure that iodine is in our multi-mineral tablets.

Daily Dosage: 15 mg.

Multi-Mineral Capsules. Instead of bothering with a separate pill for each daily mineral, I use a good multi-mineral capsule, making sure it contains all the above. But for many minerals, it is still necessary to take the extra tablets separately and in addition. Study the contents. (Iron is the one exception, as stated above).

One Final Word on Supplements

If you are allergic to yeast, artificial colorings or flavorings, be sure that what you buy in the health food store contains none. Read the labels! Even if you do not know of any reaction to these additivies, it is safer to steer clear of them. It took me years of experimentation and self-analysis to discover that the last culprit in my conquering of candida albicans (intestinal yeast infection, a chronic and severe diarrhea) was the brewer's yeast in which many of my vitamins were based.

Each Person is Different

Every person has entirely different nutrient requirements from another. Dr. Giller leads you through the intricate maze of individual health history, family background, eating and smoking habits, laying it out so clearly and accurately that you can't miss. If you never read another book, do consult *Medical Makeover!*

Healthy and Happy Living!

Extra reading on vitamins:

The B Vitamins: Their Major Role in Maintaining Your Health, Leonard Mervyn, B.Sc., Ph.D., Thorsons Publishers Ltd., 1981 (England)

Cancer and Vitamin C, Linus Pauling, Ph.D. and Ewan Cameron, M.D., W.W. Norton and Co., New York, 1979. A discussion of the nature, causes, prevention and treatment of cancer, with special reference to the value of vitamin C.

Complete Book of Vitamins, Editors of *Prevention*, Rodale Press, 1977.

Complete Guide to Anti-Aging Nutrients, Sheldon Saul Hendler, M.D., Ph.D. Simon and Schuster, New York, 1984. "Excellent guide to a balanced and useful approach to the entire question of food supplements." —Norman Cousins.

Dr. Wright's Guide to Healing With Nutrition, Jonathan V. Wright, M.D., Rodale Press, 1984

God and Vitamins, Marjorie Holmes, Avon, New York, 1980. How exercise, diet and faith can change your life. Valuable information.

How to Live Longer and Feel Better, Linus Pauling, W. H. Freeman and Co., 1986

Mega-Nutrition, Richard A. Kunin, M.D., New American Library, New York, 1980. The diet-plus-vitamins program to prevent disease, treat illness, promote good health.

Selenium as Food and Medicine, Dr. Richard A. Passwater, Keats Publishing, 1980. The remarkable mineral that protects you — and why you may not be getting enough of it.

Vitamin B-17, Michael Culbert, Arlington House Publishers,

New Rochelle, NY, 1974. The fight for laetrile, forbidden weapon against cancer.

Vitamin C and the Common Cold, Linus Pauling, W. H. Freeman and Co., 1970. It *works*, despite what the medical and pharmaceutical interests say!

Vitamin E: Key to Youthful Longevity, Raymond F. Bock, M.D., Arco Publishing Co., New York, 1977. You can live longer and better with the help of miracle-working vitamin E.

Vitamin E: The Vitality Vitamin, Dr. Leonard Mervyn. Thorsons Publishers Ltd., Wellingborough, Northamptonshire, England, 1981

Vitamins, Your Memory and Mental Attitude, Rodale Press, 1977.

How do I love thee? Let me count the ways.
—Elizabeth Barrett Browning

13. LOVE IS THE SECRET

New Life for the Maestro

Take the case of Kurt Herbert Adler, veteran maestro of the San Francisco Opera. At 60 he had struck a low in his life.

He had lost his wife and was facing possible retirement from a job he adored. What was left?

In a surprise denouement of plot which left San Francisco's opera buffs gasping, he married a 20-year-old girl who was 40 years his junior. "No fool like an old fool," laughed some. But it was the best thing that ever happened to him. After fifteen years of a happy marriage, little Sabrina Sif was born. The Maestro's directing bloomed anew, as he continued to produce his greatest operas — and a second child.

He lived a full joyful 23 years of marriage before he finally succumbed at the age of 83.

The Lovers' Litany

Two lonely old people met in a creative writing workshop; both were white-haired, with faces well-sculpted by many years of living. He was a burly retired policeman who wrote of his adventures as a cop, she a fragile little lady who had written a cookbook but aspired to write something more exciting.

The entire class cheered when Dexter Mast and Minu surprised the world with the announcement of their engagement. They were married November 22, 1980.

I wish you could see them today, blooming with a second youth. Love creates magic radiance in people, which shines out and warms those around them. That glow, even after eight years of marriage, still invites everyone who knows Dexter and Minu into its magic circle.

They have become very active in the church since their wedding. Minu sings in the choir, which has two rehearsals a week, requiring Dexter to drive many long miles from their residence in another city. But he is proud of Minu, and loves sharing her music with her. Both participate wholeheartedly in church seminars, potluck suppers, neighborhood networks, and in developing the church retreat in the hills where members have built a large geodesic-domed structure to house seminars, over-nights, and church picnics. All are activities which they had not had before they married.

Writing is another interest which they still share. They never miss a workshop of the California's Writers' Club, and attend most of the dinner meetings. They were excited last week about the meeting of the Mystery Writers of America which they had just attended. Their new-found energy is amazing.

When Dexter and I worked together at the church's Christmas Fair, he recited a poem by Kipling with which he had wooed Minu, expressing their love:

The Lover's Litany
Sing, for Faith and Hope are high—
None so true as you and I—
Sing the Lovers' Litany—
"Love like ours can never die!"

Never Too Late

Peg Chase was a vivacious beauty who taught art at Lowell High School in San Francisco — but with a yearning for adventure. On a year's sabbatical in South America, she was in Buenos Aires when Europe exploded into World War II.

As Margaret (Peg) tells so vividly in her book, *Never Too Late*, she soon managed to get herself into the thick of things via the American Red Cross, and for the duration she lived in the heart of the bombing in London, and later in North Africa as part of General Eisenhower's offical "family."

But the best part of her story comes as the book ends. Her cat Orlando was the Cupid that brought her romance — at the age of 52. Margaret's sliding doors were always open to San Francisco's breezes in those days. Orlando slept on her bed until about 3 AM and then slipped out — to spend the rest of the night with a handsome bachelor in the flat below. When the two "owners" finally met and discovered that they shared the same cat, love bloomed.

For almost nine years they carried on a secret and passionate love affair, sometimes upstairs, sometimes down.

Giovanni Camajani was the answer to any woman's dream, a distinguished-looking Italian tenor, the voice coach for the San Francisco Opera. When he went away to teach at a distant university they decided to tie the knot. They simply couldn't be separated.

Margaret was 60, Giovanni 55. But age didn't matter. Love was the thing. It wasn't until they got passports for a trip to Italy that she discovered he was exactly her age. (Theatre people in those days chopped off at least five years from their age.) They were married for 20 glorious years. Every moment was a joy.

Sex Is Great But...

It needn't be sexual love to be joyful and rejuvenating. In my nearly eight decades of living around the world, working and settling my roots on four continents, I have been blessed with scores of beautiful friends and loves, warm and deep and enriching. Of all the wonderful memories I've accumulated during this unbelievable lifetime, the most precious are of my friends.

"Life is a chronicle of friendship," wrote Helen Keller. "Friends create the world anew each day. Without their loving care, courage would not suffice to keep hearts strong for life."

Just receiving unexpected letters from Japan or Africa or Sweden keeps each day exciting. You can give without loving, but you can't love without giving, I find. It's this interflow of love across the miles, across the telephone lines, across the widest oceans, that keeps my life lively. A birthday card from Santiago or Quito or Shiraoka-machi makes the day an adventure. My friends and I (and the postal department) profit immeasurably by these stimulating contacts.

Bear Hugs Work

Leo Buscaglia, author of *Love*, a splendid book on the importance of love in our lives, took a poll on the ten most important elements of love in human relations.

"Communication" was the number one choice; "Affection" was number two. "Sex" came out way at the bottom of the list.

It's great, but it isn't all of love by a long shot.

Buscaglia feels that "touching" is an important part of true human communication. A person can stand aloof and say, "I love you." But who is to believe it? Hug people. Kiss your friends. Let them feel your human warmth. Let them feel the reality of your affection. "A hug is the perfect gift — one size fits all and nobody minds if you exchange it." (Ivera Ball)

Last Christmas we visited a couple who had been dear, dear friends for over 40 years. We don't see each other often, and in saying our farewells, Cecil gave me a bear hug that I'll never forget. It broke a rib! Who would have thought that he had just celebrated his 80th birthday? Every time I took a deep breath for the next few weeks, I remembered how much I loved Cecil and Ruby.

I Love Old People

The older the better, but only if they think young. Only if they have a lively curiosity about life.

I was introduced at a church dinner recently as a "writer." The people at my table were obviously well advanced in years.

"What do you write?" asked one.

"Well," I laughed, for I realized most of us were about the same age, "right now I'm writing a book called *How To Stay Young Forever!*"

"Good heavens!" was the response. "Who wants to? I'm looking forward to death. And the sooner, the better!"

"Me too," said another. "I'm just waiting for the good

Lord to call me."

The conversation dropped like a rock, while they munched their lunches in sad silence, like dutifully chastised children. (It was not my church, the Unitarian, where every day is an adventure.)

Love is Better than Medicine

"All patients," says Dr. Siegel, "need not wait helplessly for artificial aids. They can learn to heal themselves and stay well. If I can teach you how to feel good about your life, love yourself and others, and achieve peace of mind, the necessary changes can occur. My loving and hugging may look silly on the ward, but they're scientific... One day I hope we can prescribe something like 'one hug every three hours' instead of a drug."

God is Love

I have never been one to talk a lot about God. My religion and philosophy are centered on the deeply held belief that life and the universe are not simply the product of "the Big Bang." I do believe in the Big Bang and protons and electrons and all the rest of science.

But there is more to it that that. Did you ever look deep into the heart of night blooming cereus? They are too intricately beautiful not to have been designed by some Master Designer. A Designer who loved His art, His work. They couldn't have just popped out of the Big Bang.

One day I suddenly realized that God is love — literally! Love creates us. Love cures us. Love created the glorious world in which we live. Love performs miracles.

Cats Et Cetera

Wonderful and life-sustaining love is not limited to people, who are sometimes not available to us when we really need them. That's when pets come into their glory. Some of us love cats, some of us love dogs.

My precious companion is Princess Sheherazade, a beautiful Himalayan cat, with the long fluffy fur of a Persian and the markings of a Siamese. She is of great assistance to me in my writing, sleeping protectively nearby, and following me from room to room when I leave the typewriter. Her favorite time is when I lie on the couch in front of the TV at news time. She hops up and curls up on top of me in a wink, purring gratefully. Her bad times are when I go off on trips and leave her to be cared for by neighbors. But my homecoming is a celebration. Her love makes my life the richer.

"Love makes the world go 'round" is not just an old adage, but a vital fact of life — and health, and happiness. Give yours away! The effect is miraculous.

More about love:

Gracie, A Love Story, George Burns, Putnam, New York, 1988. A love story that carries George Burns' youth up into his 90s.

Love, Leo Buscaglia, Fawcett-Crest, New York, 1972. A warm, wonderful book about the largest experience in life.

Love is Letting Go of Fear, Gerald G. Jampolsky, M.D., Celestial Arts

Love, Medicine and Miracles, Bernie S. Siegel, M.D., Harper and Row, New York, 1986. Love can perform miracles of healing, according to this inspiring book.

The Well Cat Book, Terri McGinnis, D.V.M., Random House, NY, 1982. Make the most of your cat's nine lives.

14. RETIRE? WHO...ME?

When Griff retired from a wholly satisfying career in the U.S. Forest Service, most of it spent in the high green valleys of the Colorado Rockies, he looked around for something else to do. Still "young" and vigorous, he did not intend to sit in a rocking chair the rest of his life.

He enrolled in the University of Michigan in the School of Natural Resources, and in a record time of two and a half years, had earned a Ph.D. in Conservation of Natural Resources, with an almost straight "A" average. Don't tell me people's minds grow old! He graduated in a shorter time and with a better grade point average than most of his young classmates.

After graduation, Griff was hired by the brand new Department of Natural Resource Management at California Polytechnic University in San Luis Obispo. He and one other faculty member developed the department from a nucleus of 20 students in 1969, to over 400 students and eight instructors by 1977.

Ruth, too, bloomed in a new career. Up until then, the largest group she had faced was a class of elementary school children. Now she found herself elected president of the Cal Poly's Women's Club, with over 250 adults to manage. To her astonishment, she discovered latent administrative talents — in the first organization she had ever belonged to. She loved it!

Her hobby of giving dramatic reviews (one-woman

shows) of books and plays, came into full bloom. She performed at women's clubs, service clubs, even at a church centennial celebration. She edited books and Broadway musicals, "leaving just the juicy parts I liked to do, then tried to make all the characters come alive by taking their voices and singing their songs — usually six of them with several changes of costume and sometimes a dance or two."

They both found themselves, in their "retirement," the busiest they had ever been. Too busy, actually. So Griff retired again, at age 67.

Then he got a call from Kansas State University to teach Urban Forestry. Like a conditioned fire-horse, he leaped back into the harness and was off again. But this was a shorter stint, and they finally settled down in their "dream home" in the mountains.

But in Durango they didn't really retire. Griff is active on the Animas Water Board, serves on the city Forestry Board, is a very active member of the Lions Club (where he put in an eleven-hour shift at the Health Fair, at age 78), and is an active member of the Society of American Foresters.

Ruth went back to teaching and continues her dramatic productions. She directed a very successful readers' theatre production of *Women of the San Juan* for Durango's Centennial Celebration, takes classes at the college, and is very active in Toastmaster Club, which she helped organize.

Wherever they can find music, they dance, a beautiful couple gliding over the floor. That's retirement — for the Griffs.

How Do You Feel About Retirement?

"I think it's nonsense," responded Martha Graham some years ago, when *Modern Maturity* posed this question to her. "I don't think there should be any arbitrary retirement age. How do they know a person of 25 shouldn't retire?"

A Missouri grandmother, who began at the age of 65 to record memories of her childhood on the Missouri prairie for her grandchildren, found she would write nine bestsellers for children by the age of 90. That grandmother was Laura Ingalls Wilder, author of *The Little House on the Prairie*, which later became one of the biggest TV hits NBC ever produced.

Busy as a Beaver

"You have to have something to make you want to get out of bed in the morning," says George Burns, who at 94 is one of the busiest people in Hollywood. "Look at it this way. When you wake up, get up. When you get up, do something."

Find a Purpose for Living

When Mabel King retired as an executive secretary with the Berkeley Public Schools, it didn't take her long to find a purpose.

Thousands of Americans were going to bed hungry every night — if they indeed had a bed to crawl into. And many lived in the Bay Area.

For the next three years Mabel spent full time on what was to be called the South Berkeley Community Church Hunger Project. Working with other members of the church, she wrote application after applicaton for grants, with a starting goal of $50,000.

Mabel's application for a United Way Grant came through dramatically, with a $27,000 grant. The State regulations were extremely rigid, and the church had to rebuild the kitchen to meet their inspections, necessitating raising $30,000. It wasn't easy, those three years of persistent effort. They made up the difference through private donations, volunteer help, donated food, white elephant sales, and a gift from the United Church of Christ.

It was an uphill battle all the way, for South Berkeley Community Church was far from being a rich church, 95% black, with most of the members retired or on low incomes.

But this week the Hunger Project took off! They served their first meal on Tuesday, with 90 hungry people crowding into the dining hall. By Thursday they are expecting twice that number.

It's All in the Genes....

...Says Norma Stauffer, 92, who is busier than a beaver at dam-building time. Before retirement, she was secretary of the YWCA, working in such far-flung spots as Chicago, New Orleans, Kenya and Hawaii.

But retirement hasn't made much difference in her life. It has just given her more time to get involved in more of the organizations she cares deeply about, such as the Women's International League for Peace and Freedom.

Norma is also deeply involved in her church, taking two buses to get to services every Sunday. Her abiding passion is the promotion of understanding among the races, not only between American blacks and whites, but among other races of the world. For this reason she is extremely active in two other groups, the American Field Service and English in Action.

Her vitality is amazing. "It's all in the genes," she laughs modestly. "You have to choose the right parents. I have a lot to thank my parents for. Our family believed in being surrounded by stimulating people. I am sorry for people whose thinking is deliberately confined within themselves."

Volunteer! Volunteer! Volunteer!

Genevieve German retired 10 years ago to a strange city, a sure recipe for catastrophe for some people. Having lived in the high silences of the Andes for 15 years, she decided to retire to the bustle of Washington, D.C. But for Genevieve it has been adventure.

"I've become a volunteer at the White House one day a week. There are tons of letters received each day which have to be opened and put into slots for different categories. I've been working on requests for 50-year wedding anniversary cards. There are more than 400 volunteers.

"Pre-holiday parties are in full swing and the one yesterday at the White House for volunteers was spectacular. We were given two hours to roam the main floor rooms at will; we were served eggnog or wassail, cookies and fruit cakes.

"In the Blue Room where refreshments were served there was continuous music and singing. A beautiful inspiring experience, living for a few hours in fairyland!"

Her Passion is Peace

"My advice for staying youthful is simple," says Lucile Greene Isitt, 74, "Do something useful, preferably also important." And that is exactly what she has done — for the past 50 years. She has devoted herself with passionate dedication to working for world peace.

She led marches and rallies of the Women for Peace in the 1960s, and in 1968 she helped draft documents for the first World Constitutional Convention in Switzerland. In 1975 she was the leader in convening 500 World Citizens on the 35th anniversary of the U.N., to establish a World Citizens Assembly. She was elected President, and for the next ten years she was all over the world, organizing groups, in homes, in castles, in offices — anywhere she could get people organized for the purpose of peace. Lucile organized and was president of four World Assemblies of World Citizens. For her impassioned work, she was awarded the Gandhi Medal for Non-Violence.

Retire? Not Lucile!

So Don't Retire

Just try a new career. You may love it. Or bring out any one of the dreams you've been carrying around in your secret pocket all these years because you "didn't have time." But whatever you do, don't just retire and sit down "to rest." That's the shortest road to the funeral parlor.

Be a world citizen:

World Citizens, Dr. Lucile Greene Isitt, 774 Colusa, El
   Cerrito, CA 94530 (415) 525-5057

Sing, riding's a joy! For me I ride.
—Robert Browning

15. FUN IS FOR EVERYONE

Forgive me for my frequent quotes of Robert Browning, but the joie de vivre and eternal enthusiasm which rescued Elizabeth Barrett from a life sentence of illness still have the power, through his radiant words, to reassure us as well.

Whether you ride or whether you sing, if you do it for *fun*, it will keep you young. We call it *recreation*.

Did you ever stop to take that word apart to think what it really means? *Re-* means *again,* so *re-creation* means the act of creating again. Recreation is the process of remaking yourself through some pleasurable activity. You become a younger, healthier, happier you.

When you get the 'blahs' and are weary of the sameness of life, you can be reborn — re-created — through some kind of recreation. But it must be a recreation of your own choice to be of any good. Whether it be golf or gambling, ballet or belly-dancing, painting pansies or pigging out on pasta — whatever you do for sheer fun — do it every so often just for the hell of it. It will do you a world of good.

Life is Such Fun

I get up every morning, wondering, "What adventure will occur today?" But I don't just sit here, waiting for an adventure to drop into my lap. I hunt adventure.

I have at least one "fun" time every week. Living alone

as I do, never speaking, except to my cat, pecking away at my typewriter eight to ten hours a day, I need that fun, that connection with life and laughter and people, to keep me young and alert and healthly.

"You never stay home!" grumbles my young next-door neighbor. "On the go all the time! How do you have that much energy?"

"That's what gives me the energy," I laugh. "I'm at home, all day every day, working while you're working. You just see me driving off in the evenings or on the weekends, when I get out to have fun with my family and friends. That gives my energy a boost."

Build a Ship

Art didn't wait for retirement to begin his hobby of working with wood. He had taken a woodworking class in high school and he loved the feel of wood. On his lathe he made smoking stands and candle sticks and all kinds of bric-a-brac for Christmas presents. Then he discovered the remnants of an old model sailing ship in his step-father's woodshed. The masts were broken, the rigging badly tangled, and the whole thing practically invisible under a heavy layer of coal dust and cobwebs.

Today that trim little vessel sits proudly on Bonnie's mantle, the result of many happy hours of her father's library research, seeking detailed information on the original China Clippers, as well as many more hours spent in restoring the wreckage to its original pristine beauty.

How About a Balloon?

Bonnie felt I should enter my eighth decade with a

flourish, so she reserved a ride in a hot-air balloon. Without a doubt, the most spectacular birthday party I ever had!

The day dawned dark and stormy, with a rough sea wind coming in across the hills. When we got to the airfield, the balloon man shook his head ominously.

"Doesn't look safe. We can't take off in this."

But by 10:30 the sun had come out and the winds died down a bit. We helped with the exciting task of filling the great colorful balloon with blasts of hot air from the roaring portable furnace. At last we piled into the basket. As we eased off into the air and started to rise, the pilot warned us that our wicker basket was overloaded, four adults, a child, and the propane furnace. It was a glorious ride, floating over the California hills and valleys. But it was over all too soon.

The descent was a different story. The pilot found a likely-looking little meadow far below and pulled the rip cord, letting out the hot air with a great whoosh. We dropped toward that green target like a bat out of hell.

"Face forward!" yelled the pilot. "And hang on for all you're worth!"

As the meadow rushed up into our faces, it turned out not to be flat, but so steep as to be almost perpendicular. Then we crashed! When I regained my wits, I was in the bottom with the other passengers on top of me. It had been quite a landing. But after the champagne brunch which followed, I was ready to go again. Our crash was one in a million, our pilot assured us. Don't be afraid to try it. Ballooning is great fun!

Or Try Tahiti

That same summer, the family decided to take my eighth decade one step farther — the South Seas.

There, among the coral and sea anemones and parrot fish of Tahiti, I found another world. A world of brilliant colors and fluid movement and soft green buoyancy and sunlight filtered in jade patterns, moving, always moving. My new underwater companions swam up close to make my acquaintance a wonderful world of dazzling color. Real fun!

But You Needn't Be a Fish

There are thousands of ways of having fun, based upon your personality and your pocketbook. It needn't cost a penny. Take the College Avenue Players. Most of them had never set foot on a stage, and hadn't planned to, until young Stewart Kandell took them in hand at the Adult Activity Center in Oakland. Kandell, 37, with drama degrees from Northwestern University and the University of Newcastle in England, had the group (average age, 70) on stage, to their own astonishment and their audiences' delight.

Today they are a busy happy group of "strolling players." Kandell loads them and their props into a bus and heads out for their next production in nursing homes, libraries, museums, senior centers, hospitals, literary groups. They have even played to full houses at the Ashland Shakespeare Festival in Oregon. Kandell estimates that in the past ten years, they have played to well over 30,000 people.

Fun Comes in Many Colors

When Art Isitt retired as an engineer from Shell Oil, he wandered into a senior center one day to see "what was cooking." Now that he had time, what would he do with it?

He was intrigued by a class in oil painting and watched, fascinated. Next day he bought his own set of oils and joined the class. Today his beautiful paintings hang in his own home, as well as adorning the walls of some of his friends.

One Man Band

Art originated another fascinating form of recreation — creating his own one-man music "ensemble." He'd always loved music, but had no training except for that in elementary school, singing. His first musical experience was with a "harmonica" with a lever that could add sharps and flats.

When he retired, bought a second-hand electric chord organ, and set up a spare bedroom as a "music studio," the fun started. He got a multi-track tape recorder, and the "Art Isitt Swing Band" was born.

His repertoire of '30s, '40s, and '50s songs was extensive. Recording one track over another, he would sing the song, add the rhythms with the chord organ, add on the melody with the chromonica, and finally dub in the harmonics on the fourth track. The result is utterly delightful. Glenn Miller and Benny Goodman at their swingin' best, a good jazzy arrangement.

No Age Limit

Felix Kuhner is the oldest member of the Prometheus

Symphony Orchestra, (although that might be debate-able, as there are many splendid musicians in the group with hair as white as his). But there is little doubt that he is old enough to be the grandfather of many of the musicians there.

I love his favorite story: "I dreamed one night I was playing a viola in the San Francisco Opera orchestra. It was the opera Aida. Then I woke up. And I was!"

He had been a symphony director himself, so when he retired, there was no question in his mind what he would do "for fun." Play the viola, of course.

The charming part of this story is that Felix is espe-cially proud to be playing with Prometheus Symphony. The conductor, Jonathon Kuhner, is his son.

Shared fun is the best kind.

Have fun! Here's how to have an adventure:

College Avenue Players, 6408 Valley View road, Oakland, CA 94611. Active repertory theatre group. If you want to start such a group, write: Vista College, 2020 Milvia, Berkeley, CA 94704-1183 for info.

Colorado Trail is a recently completed hiking trail that wanders back and forth across the Continental Divide. If you're interested in hiking (not mountain-climbing), write Regional Forester, U.S. Forest Service, 11177 W. 8th Avenue, Box 25127, Lakewood, CO 80225.

Spoleto Festival USA, P.O. Box 704, Charleston, SC 29402, is an exciting fine arts festival that plays each summer, May 26 to June 11, set in the most fascinating and lovely city of the old Deep South.

Oregon Shakespeare Festival, Ashland, OR 97520, is the American way to revel in the best of the Elizabethan theatre, as well as in some of the finest of modern theatre.

Oregon Trail Wagon Train, Rt. 2, Bayard, NE 69334
(308) 586-1850 will take you on a 4-day, 3-night
covered wagon trip along the old Trail from June to
September. An historic reliving of the Old West.

Wagons Ho, Inc., Frank and Ruth Hefner, P.O. Box 60098,
Phoenix, AZ 85082 (602) 230-1801. Travel the Smoky
Hill Trail in covered wagons, stage coach, or horseback
with Trail Boss, Wranglers and Camp Cooks. (For other
groups offering such fun, see *Modern Maturity*,
May 1987, pp. 96-99.)

Triangle-T Guest Ranch, P.O. Box 218, Dragoon, AZ 85609
(602) 586-3738. Old Ranch life at its best.

Literary Journey. Get a Blake Literary Map and explore the
exact sites where some of our literary events actually
occurred. Available are *The John Steinbeck Map of
America, The Raymond Chandler Mystery Map of Los
Angeles, The Ernest Hemingway Adventure Map of the
World, The Jane Austen Map of England, The Ian
Fleming Thriller Map*, and *The Sir Arthur Conan Doyle
Mystery Map of London*. Available for $4.95 from
Aaron Blake Publishers, 1800 S. Robertson, Suite 130,
Los Angeles, CA 90035.

Measure your mind's height by the shade it casts!
—Robert Browning

16. USE YOUR HEAD

If you had to choose giving up the use of either your mind or your body, which would you choose? Most of us, I'm sure, would prefer to keep the old head clicking accurately as long as possible. But we needn't make such a choice. This book is designed to keep both mind and body operating at top efficiency much longer that was once thought possible.

Scientists have discovered that there are two distinct paths to be taken in preserving the abilities of the mind. One is physical, the other mental. One is not much good without the other. Let's first explore the physical aspects of the brain and aging.

Save Your Brain Cells

Contrary to popular belief, you do not start losing vast numbers of brain cells annually upon reaching adulthood, says Dr. Marian Diamond, neuroanatomist at U.C. Berkeley. The rapid cell loss occurs at an early age, and levels off in later years, provided you take care of that precious mechanical masterpiece, the brain. Through measurements and weights, it has been proven that the brain can actually increase in size and efficiency with the years, if cared for properly.

Brain Thief

However, there is one sure way of getting rid of some of those irreplaceable cells. It's a silent, sneaky, pleasant method that you'll never suspect — until it's too late. It's not like the robber who breaks into your house and shoots up the place while walking off with his loot. You don't see him coming. And you don't realize how much precious bounty he has gotten away with until he's been at it over the years.

It's the socially acceptable custom of drinking alcohol. Even one gin-and-tonic or a Bloody Mary robs you of a few brain cells, reducing your total count measurably.

Those stolen brain cells can never be recovered, but it's never too late to lock the barn door when only a few of your horses have been stolen. Keep those you have left.

Another Crook

Another criminal that robs you of part of that marvelous natural computer system that we call the mind, is drugs, both legal and illegal. The derelict wreckages of humanity which are the result of using "crack," "coke" and "angel dust" are too prevalent to mention. You find them everywhere, on the streets, in the parks, and what is ever more terrifying, in the work place — until they are eventually fired.

There now is no question that the smoking of marijuana damages the brain. Conclusive statistics prove that students who smoke "pot" regularly have lower overall grade point averages than before taking up the habit, or than other students with the same IQ. Marijuana is also definitely linked with lung cancer, proving to be more dangerous than tobacco. A brain doesn't function well in a body devoured by lung cancer.

Do It to Music

Lively activity increases the flow of blood to the brain, as it does to the rest of the body. Spirited actions carry oxygen to the brain, helping to prevent the fatty buildup and thickening of the nerve coverings which are inevitable to some degree in the extremely old. Activity also speeds up blood flow to carry necessary nutrients to the brain cells.

Agreed, exercise is stimulating to the brain. And now there is new evidence to show that doing that exercise to music is even more beneficial. Swim. Dance. Do aerobics. Exercising to music actually changes your pulse rate more effectively that the same exercise without it. Sex therapists even suggest that making love to music enhances the ultimate satisfaction and afterglow derived from this most natural of exercises.

Posture for Brain Power

Seems a bit farfetched, doesn't it? But it's true. E. Fritz Schmerl, M.D. (*The Challenge of Age*, Continuum, 1986), who teaches gerontology at Chabot College in Hayward, California, shows how poor posture robs the brain of its necessary blood supply.

Is your thinking getting hazy? Are you a bit dizzy and your memory fuzzy these days? Check your posture. If your shoulders are slumped forward and your chin raised, this position will put a sharp kink in your spine at the base of your skull, which in turn pinches the two arteries carrying blood to the brain. As this position continues, it can cause a buildup of fatty deposits that can cause a partial blockage.

Stand tall and straight, with your head back and your

chin in. You'll not only look younger, you'll think younger.

Perk Up with Lecithin

Lecithin (sold, incidentally, as "Pam," the vegetable cooking spray used to oil pans) is found abundantly in eggs and liver — and in the brain. In fact, the brain functions longer and more efficiently if it has an ample supply.

Dr. Diamond recommends an egg a day — to stay smart. Perhaps that's why she looks and functions as though she were 20 years younger. She practices what she preaches.

"As the brain ages," says Dr. Ronald Mervis of Ohio State University's Brain Aging Research Center, "its cell membranes become more rigid with fatty deposits and lose their ability to take in and release chemicals and to relay messages. This may cause memory loss and confused thinking."

They have proven, according to Dr. Mervis, that lechithin-fed mice are much more alert that those without.

"B" for Brain

Although we know that alcoholics have reduced mental powers and short-term memory loss, most of us don't know that people who are long on alcoholic intake are also short of vitamin B. Even non-drinkers over 60 often have poor memory and an inability to concentrate. The University of New Mexico School of Medicine in Albuquerque found that older people with even a slight subclinical deficiency of vitamin B display a markedly less than optimum metal ability.

Keep Active and Involved

Now let's look at the mental approach to stimulating the mind to keep it young.

Don't allow your mind to become drugged by the highly addictive "drug" TV. It can steal your will and your strength for doing something that will make you healthier and happier. It is something "poured" into your mind, without requiring any mental responses, and can be deadening to the brain.

Use It or Lose It

Dr. James Fries of the Stanford Medical Center believes that the body "rusts out" rather than wears out. That includes the brain, says Dr. Fries. Memory loss can be successfully resisted by exercising the brain as one exercises the body. "Mental agility in old age comes from giving the brain regular workouts. You can't fight the trend entirely," he says, "but you can greatly slow that process."

Mental Aerobics

Some people seem to have all the luck — bad! Jean Brown had fallen several times and had broken both arms. Her balance was bad, but the doctors couldn't figure out why. When she got the second cast off, she and her husband, Taylor, flew to Italy for a long-planned vacation.

In Naples she fell on the marble floor of their hotel room and broke her hip. After a noteworthly ambulance ride to Rome and a flight back to California on a stretcher (a 4-day trip without medical attention), she entered the operating room for a long surgical procedure.

While she was in the hospital, recuperating, the doctor gave her a cat-scan and discovered a brain tumor the size of a small grapefruit.

The indomitable Jean continues to be plagued by pain, but she is determined not to lose the use of her mind. Although degenerative arthritis keeps her housebound most of the time, she is as bright and cheery as ever. Never a day passes without her doing her regular mental aerobics — the crossword puzzle in the daily paper.

Elderhosteling to Stay Young

Here is one of the greatest inventions since the wheel, as a key to staying young. Just ask Louise and Spencer Prange. They Elderhosteled in Alaska not long ago, and are now excitedly planning another Elderhostel adventure to Prince Edward Island next summer.

Modeled on the youth hostels that have long been popular with students traveling in Europe, Elderhosteling has now been taken a step farther. Accessible to anyone over 60, it is a traveling-learning experience with an exhilarating array of destinations, often at universities and colleges scattered around the world, where the "students" hear lectures, take exciting field trips and attend classes in a wide variety of subjects.

During WWII Louise had been stationed in Ketchikan, while Spence was in the Aleutians. They always wanted to re-visit Alaska under more propitious circumstances, so in September, 1985, they set off for a week at $260 apiece, board, room and tuition. They couldn't have stayed in a motel at home for that price.

They came back ecstatic. They had studied at Prince William Sound Community College at Valdez, taking daily classes in Alaskan history, natural history of Alaska, and Alaskan literature. They found their classmates friendly, compatibly their own age, alert and eager to devour everything offered about this new "Land of the Midnight Sun."

Say It in French

Or Swahili. Studying a foreign language is a sure way to wake up those lazy brain cells. I was petrified with anxiety when I had to pass a French exam at U.C. Berkeley, along with all those young, high-IQ graduate students. You take French classes and pass the comprehensive exam — if you want to remain in the graduate program. You have three chances and you're out. I knew some brilliant young students who didn't make it. I was terrified. But I passed, with flying colors. At age 55!

K. Warner Schaire, Ph.D., professor of human development at Pennsylvania State University, says that the overall thinking skills of a 55-year-old are almost always markedly superior to those of a 25-year-old. He has shown that a challenged brain never quits learning.

Think You Can

The sky's the limit if you keep that "thinker" thinking. Confidence in your ability is half the battle. Too many people have been brainwashed to believe that as they grow older, they will naturally grow senile. Mooseberries! Only the truly ill, those with a vitamin deficiency, or lazy people need fear this problem.

Expect to keep that lively mind, and you'll do it!

Don't sabotage your intellectual potential by saying, "I'm too old." Keep reading good books. Learn to play the piano, as Art Anderson does. Study anthropology.

It's Never Too Late to Think Young

As Arnold Toynbee wrote, "As one grows older, the temptation is to dwell in the past...Our minds, so long as they keep their cutting edge, are not bound by physical limits; they can range over time and space into infinity. To be human is to be capable of transcending oneself."

> *Man's mind, once stretched by a new idea, never regains its original dimensions.*
> —Oliver Wendell Holmes.

To keep the mind young:

Don't Forget, Danielle C. Lapp, McGraw-Hill, New York, 1987. Easy exercises for a better memory at any age.

Elderhostel, Inc., Dept. M., P.O. Box 1721, Wakefield, MA 01880. Go "back to school" with other seniors in some of the most stimulating sites in the world.. Send for their exciting catalog.

Vitamins, Your Memory and Your Mental Attitude, Rodale Press, Emmaus, PA, 1977. Is it senility — or vitamin deficiency? Here's the answer.

Fifty is young for a tree, mid-life for an elephant,
and ancient for a quarter-miler. Fifty is a nice number
for the states in the Union or for a national speed limit,
but not a number I was prepared to have hung on me
—Bill Cosby

17. THE BEST MEDICINE

"A laugh a day keeps the doctor away." And now there's scientific proof of this old motto, and why it works. We've known for a long time that people who can laugh, or who can make others laugh, are a lot more fun to be around than woebegone doom-sayers. But as for laughter actually being good medicine...?

Dr. Bernie Siegel tells us that there are sound scientific reasons why we call a good old-fashioned belly-laugh "hearty." "It producers complete, relaxed action of the diaphragm, exercising the lungs, increasing the blood's oxygen level, and gently toning the entire cardiovascular system...After the laughter, all the muscles are relaxed, including the heart — the pulse rate and blood pressure decline... Physiologists have found that muscle relaxation and anxiety cannot exist together."

Scientists have found that laughter increases the production of the brain chemicals, catecholamines, which can reduce inflammation by activating the immune system. These chemicals also stimulate the production of endorphins, the body's natural opiates. So by this complex process, a good laugh really can kill your pain, activate your immune system, and reduce inflammation, while at the same time diverting you into a state of relaxation.

Pregnant?

An 84-year-old women was feeling a bit woozy in the mornings, so she went to see her doctor. He examined her and told her she was pregnant. She immediately called her 93-year-old boy friend and told him the news. He turned up his hearing aid and said, "Who did you say this is?"

That's one of Norman Cousins' favorites. Cousins, as you know, is now on the staff of UCLA Medical School, because of his well-documented self-cure of the "fatal" disease, ankilosing spondylitis, and his theories on the benefits of laughter, described in his book, *Anatomy of an Illness* (Norton, 1979). When he was stricken with this agonizing collagen disease (which Cousins terms "coming unglued") in 1964, specialists told him he had a 1-in-500 chance of recovery.

He decided to take his own health in hand. He ordered large quantities of vitamin C to be administered intravenously, in spite of his doctor's opposition. He left the hospital and checked into a hotel. There he surrounded himself with Marx Brothers comedies, *Candid Camera* classics, stacks of rib-tickling books — and plenty of vitamin C.

He discovered that "ten minutes of genuine belly laughter had an anesthetic effect and would give at least two hours of pain-free sleep."

He laughed over writing some "spoofs" for *The Saturday Review*, of which he had been editor for many years. One of these tells of a computer error that resulted in the manufacture of 47,000 razor blades with scalloped edges, and offered prizes for suggestions for the best use for scalloped razor blades. The agony began to subside. Eventually he was completely cured.

Small wonder that Norman Cousins was wooed by four medical schools before he decided on UCLA. Laughter *is* the best medicine.

A final Cousins story: An 94-year-old man married a 22-year-old bride. Troubled, he called his doctor. "I understand your difficulties," interrupted the doctor with soothing words.

"But it's not what you think, Doc," said the old gentleman. "That part is going fine. It's just that I can't remember her name."

Start Wearing Purple

Some people are born solemn. It's in their genes. Their worlds are pretty gloomy. Others are born with laugh bubbles inside them, like uncorked champagne, ready to erupt. Who would you rather meet? Who will have the longest and happiest life? You're right! The bubble people.

But if you're the solemn type, you can learn to loosen up a big, *look* for humor in things. It's around you everywhere. The absurdities of human nature are limitless. True, the world can be a pretty gloomy place, but it won't help the situation any for you to grump about it. *Do* something about it, but don't be Gloomy Gus while you're doing it. Laugh, tell a joke, and you'll get more people on your side of the argument. How do you think Reagan remained so popular? His eternal laughter made people *feel* good, despite his political faux pas.

My young 84-year-old friend, Dorothy Wither, whose

laughter bubbled up like a fountain, sent me this poem shortly before her death. If you knew Dorothy and her impeccable taste (she owned a swanky dress shop), this poem would seem even funnier:

When I Am an Old Woman

I shall wear purple
With a red hat which doesn't go, and doesn't suit
*   me,*
And I shall spend my pension on brandy and
*   summer gloves*
And satin sandals, and say we've no money for
*   butter.*
I shall sit on the pavement when I'm tired
And gobble up samples in shops and press alarm
*   bells*
And run my stick along public railings
And make up for the sobriety of my youth.
I shall go out in my slippers in the rain
And pick flowers in other people's gardens
And learn to spit...
But maybe I ought to practice a little now?
So people who know me are not too shocked and
*   surprised*
When suddenly I am old and start to wear purple.

—Jenny Joseph

How to Live to Be 100

This is the title of George Burns' fourth book, published when he was 87. The book is dedicated to the widows of his last six doctors. How does he do it? He laughs. He had open-heart surgery many years ago, but today he is running full steam ahead. He gets around like a young man, hears well, and answers even better.

If he goes on playing God, as he did so successfully in his last two films, he just may go on forever. What is God like?

"He should be kind," George wrote his agent, "wise, witty, sympathetic, and he could use more humorous epigrams."

He should know. He's 94 and getting closer to God every day, despite his dry martini lunch and his cigars. Laughter does it. That's why he loved his friend, Jack Benny.

"He never stopped laughing," says George. "He made me feel like I was nine feet tall. In fact, he had me so convinced I almost became a basketball player." (From *Dr. George Burns' Prescription for Happiness*.)

The Neighbor's Bull

A favorite friend was Ferry Carpenter, Princeton-lawyer-turned-cowboy-rancher, and raconteur par excellence. As long as he lived, I never went to Colorado without driving out to his ranch for a visit. He was balm to the soul, with a wit that set the world right once more.

One of his best stories tells of the time when he and another young university man took up a homestead in the Rockies, and began breeding cattle of an exceptionally high quality, which they could sell at premium prices.

A neighboring rancher had a bull with a passionate yen for Ferry's cows. But this common range bull, breeding with the "high society" cows of the young entrepreneurs, was ruining their business. So Ferry called on the rancher and asked him to keep his bull off the range at breeding time. He found the old boy anything but friendly. In fact, the gun pointed in Ferry's direction made him seem downright hostile.

The next time the young fellows found the bull in their herd of cows, they roped and castrated him. They thoughtfully replaced his natural organs with a china door knob which they had bought for their new cabin, and carefully sewed up the incision. That was the end of their problems. I can still hear Ferry chuckling, at age 94.

You're Only Old Once

Dr. Seuss, who has kept generations of children giggling and haw-hawing for the past 50 years with his delightful books of wit and whimsy, has recently written a new one, *You're Only Old Once*, this one designed for the geriatric set, of which he is one.

Theodore Seuss Geisel, otherwise known to millions as our beloved "Dr. Seuss," dedicated his new book, "With affection for and affliction with the Members of the Class of 1925." He is only 86 himself, and has laughed his way through every year of his life. He has been awarded the Pulitzer Prize Citation, two Emmys and a Peabody Award — just for making people laugh. And three films that he wrote won Academy Awards.

In this recent book, he turns his gentle guns on himself — and his visit to the medical clinic. Dr. Seuss describes it as a book "for obsolete children." "Is this a children's book?/ Well... not immediately./ You buy a copy for your child now/and give it to him on his 70th birthday."

Call at your bookstore and get a copy (Random House, 1986). You'll laugh all the way home.

You're Not Getting Older, You're Getting Better

So says Dr. Joyce Brothers, but Bill Cosby says she's "the kind of doctor who inspires a second opinion." He goes on to say in his own book, *Time Flies* (Dolphin/Doubleday, 1987), "Getting older, of course, is a distinctly better change than the one that brings you eulogies...The poet, Robert Browning, considers it the best change of all:

> *Grow old along with me!*
> *The best is yet to be.*

"On days when I need aspirin to get out of bed, Browning is clearly a minor poet; but he was an optimist and there is always comfort in his lines, no matter how much you ache."

In his delightful book, written to celebrate his 50th birthday, Cosby recounts his efforts to recover his once magnificent athletic powers. "Needless to say, the odds on my succeeding were almost as good as the odds on a bullfighter loosing his ear to a bull."

Laughter Is Better Than Aspirin

I know. I've used it for years — long before Norman Cousins wrote his remarkable book. My back would be aching, my head would be aching, my varicose veins would be aching. After a good hearty laugh, I always noticed that the pain would be gone. So I would deliberately think of something funny (like the night I tried to rush through the bathroom door — without opening it). It always worked. And I'd never heard of endorphins.

Anything for a laugh!

Look for laughter:

For information on the role laughter plays in health, write:
Alison Craine, Executive Director,
American Association for Therapeutic Humor,
9040 Forestview Rd.,
Skokie, IL 60203-1913.

For a list of humor tapes and books, write:
Leonard Reinhard, Coordinator,
Golub Humor Program,
Sunnyview Rehabilitation Hospital,
Schenectady, NY 12305.

The Cosby Wit: His Life and Humor, Bill Adler, Lorevan
Publishing Co., New York, 1986. A behind-the-scenes
look at an American phenomenon with Cosby humor
you've never heard before. A book for everyone who
loves laughter.

Dr. Burns' Prescription for Happiness, George Burns,
Putnam, 1984. Laugh with the nonagenarian actor,
writer and comedian.

How To Live To Be 100 or More, George Burns, New
American Library, New York, 1983. Do it—with
laughter.

Time Flies, Bill Cosby, Doubleday, New York, 1987. This
humorist and educator's views on aging.

You're Only Old Once! Dr. Seuss, Random House, 1986.
What Dr. Seuss did for generations of children, he
now does for seniors — makes us laugh. He can,
because he is one himself. Hilarious.

I shall pass through this world but once. Any good, therefore, I can do, any kindness I can show any human being, let me do it now. Let me not defer or neglect it — for I shall not pass this way again.
— William Penn

18. MAKE YOUR DAY

You wake up to a wet, sodden gray sky, draped over the rooftops like a dirty dishrag. You flip on the TV for something to relieve the gloom. It's the news — with detailed reports of a rape, a spate of robberies right here in town, a murder in your own bank, hopeless wars and bombings in Central America and Israel, and more blazing ships sunk in the Persian Gulf. You snap off the TV. The whole world is a bloody mess — and nothing you can do about it. Makes you want to go back to bed and stay there the rest of your life, doesn't it?

Hell, no! Not me! Nor thousands of others who don't take it lying down. You can make your own day. Make it full and beautiful and wonderful — and in so doing, make it a wonderful day for others. It's not true that there's nothing you can do about it.

You Can Make a Difference

For many years Mary Elizabeth Gillespie has worked for peace — through her church, the United Nations, and every other organization which offered a way. She didn't know that anyone noticed. Then last May, at the nadir of her life (she was struggling with chemotherapy, trying to recover from severe abdominal surgery for cancer), she received a citation from The

Rocky Mountain Conference encompassing the combined churches of Colorado, Utah and Wyoming. "Hope for a better future is exactly what you have given to so many people.

"Your efforts have touched many and made their lives better. Your love and concern have warmed our hearts and made them overflow."

And then, just a year later, with her recovery well along, she received a personal invitation from the United Nations to participate in their Peace Conference in New York in June as a VIP spectator.

"I didn't even know they knew who I was!" she says in awed modesty.

A Useless Life is an Early Death — Goethe

Genevieve was an attractive friend who worked in the American Consulate in Guayaquil. Early one morning, she was knocked down by a thug in front of the Consulate and her wrist watch stolen. Her arm was broken. Although she had lived in Ecuador for 17 years, she decided it was time to return to the United States. She loved Ecuador and its proud, poor people, but she had had enough. When she finally realized the vast extent of her dead husband's estate, in *fincas* and landholdings in Ecuador valued at several million dollars, she made a decision.

She would found a technical agricultural institute on one of her fincas near Quito, and put it under the management of Monsignor Romero, a noted educator in Ecuador. Soon there were 150 indigenous students enrolled, to be trained at the secondary level in Agricultural Science and Dairy Farming.

Two years later she was summoned back to Quito to receive a Medal and Scroll from Pope John Paul II at a special ceremony. Amid military bands, flying flags, TV cameras, and throngs of dark-skinned people, this tall classic blue-eyed blonde was honored by an hour-long ceremony at the Mayor's Palace in Machichi, and later was feted at a private champagne reception at the old hacienda, now renamed the Instituto Agropecuario Genoveva German. "They really made me feel as if I were 'Queen for a Day'...It was a good and very warm feeling to know that I was going to be able to help some of those throngs of people who are much less fortunate than I am."

Our Daily Bread

Thank God there are people like Carolyn North, founder of the "Daily Bread Project" in Berkeley. She and her crew of volunteers pick up surplus food from grocery stores, restaurants, bakeries, and university dining halls, and distribute it directly to free-food kitchens. How much does the project cost? $0.00.

"The Daily Bread Project," Carolyn told the editor of *Regeneration* newsletter, "was created to address the dual problems of local hunger and local waste. By intercepting food which is ordinarily thrown out at the end of the business day and bringing the surplus to soup kitchens, shelters and refuges, we hoped to have a variety of effects in the community: 1. feeding more people for less; 2. preventing waste of nutritious food; 3. educating the public about hunger and waste; 4. providing means for individuals to actively combat world hunger. Our challenge was to accomplish this with no full-time staff and no budget.

"The community aspect of the project is vital and it's also the most fun. That's the key to the equation: Fun! It has to be a pleasure in order to work. The pleasure in meeting people is not really the gravy of our work, it is the essence of it."

"Cast Thy Bread Upon the Waters....

....And it shall be returned to you a thousandfold."

Not real bread, necessarily, the kind that goes so well with butter, but metaphorical bread — sustenance, love, caring. Visit someone in a nursing home, someone who has no caring family to visit him or her regularly. At first it may sadden you, and terrify you with the hopelessness of it. But you will find how eagerly the residents will await your visits, and how joyfully they will respond.

Sunshine

"Those who bring sunshine into the lives of others cannot keep it from themselves," wrote the Scottish playwright, James Barrie, author of *Peter Pan*. There are thousands of ways of bringing that sunshine, while basking in its radiant warmth yourself. The ways are as varied as your imagination will go. Look at your own God-given talents. What can you share?

Susan Thompson, long retired, writes lovely, lilting, gracious little notes to her friends on every and any occasion. Just to receive an envelope with Susan's name in the corner lifts my spirits for the day. She is also an inveterate "clipper." During her reading of the daily paper, she invariably finds something that she knows will be of interest to someone she knows. So she reads with scissors at hand, and enriches someone else's day in the process.

Helen Crickmay, 80, teaches burglars and drug addicts to read. She is coordinator of a volunteer tutoring program at Orange County's minimum security jail.

"Aren't you afraid?" she is asked. "Heavenly days, no!" she responds. "They are so eager to learn to read, they love to see us coming. All their lives they have been unable to read signs and newspapers, and they are desperate to overcome this terrible handicap. And their progress is remarkable —much better than when they were forced to go to school. Some of these men advance as much as one grade level in a month. It's very exciting."

One of my greatest joys is harvesting some 75 pounds of oranges from the big orange tree in my back yard each year. It's not easy to climb to the top of a 10-foot stepladder and crawl through the tangled branches to grasp those elusive out-of-reach oranges. And climbing back down, carrying a heavy bucket full of fruit, takes a bit of courage for a certain small 79-year-old. Especially if I happen to glance down and see the cement far below.

But when I load bags and bags of oranges into my car and take them to the Richmond Rescue Mission, the joy and welcome on those wonderful faces makes it an adventure.

Let Every Day Be Christmas

Christmas is the one time of the year when the whole world glows with the warmth of giving, when people smile at one another on the street and call out, "Merry

Christmas!" across their armloads of packages. It is the season of Love.

Can we bring the warmth of Christmas into every day of the year? Let's allow life to expand and take on an added dimension by thinking of the needs of others, by showing, through word and deed, that we are really bigger than that tight little skin we were born with.

The Art of Giving

Rosella Palmer's gift is that of exquisite calligraphy. Her productions are a feast for the senses, a graceful, lilting kind of music that we can "hear" through our eyes.

On my study wall hangs a framed selection called *The Art of Giving*, by Wilfred A. Peterson, product of Rosella's pen. Here is part of it:

The Art of Giving

The gifts of things are never as precious as the gifts of thought. Emerson said it well: "Rings and jewels are not gifts but apologies for gifts. The only true gift is a portion of thyself."

You'll never grow old if you give yourself away!

To help make your day:

Habitat for Humanity International, Millard Fuller, Habitat and Church Streets, Americus, GA 31709. Write to see how you can help build homes for the homeless. This is Jimmy and Roseland Carter's lifelong project.

For a copy of Jack Kidd's program, *Working for Disarmament,* write: Route 1, Box 780A, Earlysville, VA 22936, and ask for "Star Light."

The Great Peace March, Franklin Folsom, P.O. Box 507, Boulder, CO 80306. Send $10.95 + $1.50 shipping for a copy and become inspired by this man's passion.

Loving Life, Helen Hays, Doubleday, New York, 1987.

Boot, saddle, to horse, and away!
—Robert Browning

19. I DARE YOU!

You'll know that you're rapidly approaching old age when you are afraid to try something new — a new food, a new way of looking at something, a new place to go for vacation — just because you haven't tried it before.

Chronological age has nothing to do with it. I have a teenaged grandson who is quite senile at times. Try a new food? Gosh, no! It might be poison. Or at best it might make him sick. Well...not sick exactly. But...*maybe* he wouldn't like it. But I have hopes of his out-growing his senility. His mother is working on it.

Youth is the Ability to Accept a Challenge

It was almost midnight when the phone rang. It was a friend with the offer of a two-year contract to teach in Japan. I was 55, married, working on a graduate degree at UC-Berkeley, and grandmother of one and a half grandchildren. Would I go? I considered the matter carefully for about a half a second. Of course! Who would turn down a chance like that?

I'll admit now that all those negative factors I've just mentioned never entered my mind at the time. I've never been one to consider the negatives, to think of age, nor to hesitate. Since my beautiful and exciting experience in Japan, I've accepted many such challenges to teach abroad, all upon invitation. And never once have I regretted my hasty decisions.

162

Be Outrageous

Frances McClatchy had always wanted to see Switzerland at Christmas time. Maybe as a child she had seen pictures of Yule logs and evergreens, and mountains of white snow around quaint fairy-tale houses, with the Alps towering all around. Now that she was 86, she wouldn't make the trip any younger. She'd go, by jingo!

With three children, six grandchildren, and five great-grandchildren, it might be hard to get away. They all made such a big deal of Christmas, and made a great fuss over "Grammy." Did she dare? Yet that travel brochure was most alluring.

She went. But she didn't go alone. To her surprise, daughter Winona leaped at the thought of going with her. And so while the family frolicked in the familiar snowbanks of Colorado, "Big Grammy" and "Little Grammy" were frolicking in the old-world villages of the Swiss Alps, watching the yule dancers and listening to Christmas yodelers.

Spontaneity Is Youth

When our daughters were in high school, I got the mumps. I had been immune, both as a child and when my children had them, but now in my 40s I succumbed. Because of the danger of encephalitis, my doctor insisted that I stay in bed for ten days — a life sentence for me.

The first evening I was up for dinner, I suggested that we leave the next day for the Deep South to see the Confederate Pageant and the Azalea Trail Festival. All eyes turned to me, terrified. Mom had lost her mind!

None of us had ever been South — or East. And the next day?

It was insane. But during my prolonged bed rest I had been poring over magazines which, by coincidence, all featured the lures of the Old South in early March. And the snowbanks around our house were getting deeper. I had my plans all primed and ready, so it didn't take the family long to agree that it was a daring but delightful idea.

Then the girls cried out in sudden anguish.

"Oh, the band contest! We have to practice! Mr. Flanders will never let us go in a thousand years! Not now...just before the music contest."

"I'll take care of Mr. Flanders. You girls go and talk to your other teachers. We're going."

Go we did. With the promise, made in blood, that the girls would practice their instruments for at least an hour every day during the two weeks that we would be gone.

I called Grandpa in Denver. Would he like to go along? Hell, yes! Nearing 80, he was still not one to turn his back on a good dare.

"I'll be packed by the time you get here," he promised.

It's a good thing the old gentleman was stone deaf in one ear. That way he suffered only half the racket of both girls practicing simultaneously in the back seat of the car as we tootled cross-country, Grandpa sitting in the middle. Sharon played the French horn and Bonnie the bassoon.

"How are you coming?" I called back to Gramp.

"Cheap at half the price!" he shouted back, grinning.

Flexibility keeps you young.

Do the Unthinkable

"You will do foolish things," said the French writer, Colette, "but do them with enthusiasm." Obey some of those wild impulses that occur to you. You'll never be sorry, for your life will only be the richer for it.

Horowitz's father, who lived on Music Street in Kiev, once was so excited upon hearing Pablo Casals play in a concert, he rushed out and bought a cello, which he never learned to play. But he had no regrets. His passion for music was so infectious, it permeated his young son to the core. Perhaps that is one of the reasons Horowitz was to become one of the world's greatest pianists.

Don't put limits on yourself. Like "What will people think?"

You can achieve things, if you believe you can do it. Dare to dare! Take risks that help you grow.

Be Adventurous

One of the most accurate Chinese fortune cookies I ever opened says, "Life for you is a bold and dashing adventure."

How did they know? I keep it taped to my filing cabinet, just in case things get slow. At a moment's notice, I'm ready for anything. I always keep my bags packed, just in case...

As a result I've lived all over the world, Nicaragua, Ecuador, Mexico, France, Japan, England, Austria, Italy. Just give me a ticket and I'll go anywhere. I'll also do other insane things — like riding out a devastating typhoon alone in Japan, or running down a murder in the moldy catacombs of the dead under the cathedral in Quito, or riding a runaway horse on a bull ranch in Mexico or a raft down the wild water of Lodore Canyon (all *after* middle age).

I dare you to stay young forever!

Others who dared:

The Day I Owned the Sky, Robert Lee Scott, Jr., Brigadier General, USAF (Retired), Bantam Books, New York, 1988. The account of a daring life in the US Air Force, by the author of *God Is My Co-Pilot*.

In The Autumn Wind, Dorothy Stroup, Scribner, New York, 1986. A remarkably moving and beautiful novel of the bombing of Hiroshima, from the viewpoint of a Japanese mother. A story of daring courage and love, by an American woman who dared to go alone to Japan to live.

Never Too Late, Margaret Chase, Ausonia Press, 100 Thorndale Drive, #457, San Rafael, CA 94903 ($12 + $1.50 shipping). Autobiography of a daring young teacher who leaped into WWII by joining the Red Cross in the British and North African theatre, becoming intimately acquainted with Eisenhower, Patton, Kay Summersby and Randolph Churchill. She fell in love at 65 and married an Italian tenor.

Great wide, beautiful, wonderful world,
With the wonderful water round you curled,
And the wonderful grass upon your breast,
World, you are so beautifully dressed!
—Matthew Browne

20. FEAST ON BEAUTY

The Christmas that I was in the second grade, I received a gift of beauty, an exquisitely illustrated book of nursery rhymes. Any book was a treasure on that isolated homestead, for we had so few of them, but this one, in full color, captured my heart. Some of the rhymes were familiar, but some were new to me. In a short time I knew them all by heart, reading them over and over.

The above rhyme was my favorite, and I have said it ten thousand times since...every time I am confronted with a breath-taking view of the Golden Gate with the sun sinking into a bank of crimson behind it, or catch the sudden green vision of the Yampa Valley spread below Rabbit Ear Pass. My soul is transported by the wondrous luminosity of nature.

Seek beauty. It is around us everywhere, but so few of us take the time to look, to savor it. We are too busy looking down to look up!

You Can't Buy Beauty

But you can have it for free. Every time you open your eyes to beauty — really look — you will be letting a song of gratitude into your heart. Every time you allow some of the mysterious loveliness around you to enter your consciousness, you will transcend the ugly life that makes cynics, and for a glorious moment of euphoria, you will find joyous perfection. If you've never felt this electric jolt at the sight of beauty, I'm afraid I can't describe it to you. But it's worth more than all the mind-altering drugs you can buy. And it is beneficial to the health.

That's what I love about Japan — the people's love for beauty. For centuries those islands were a land of gentile poverty. Almost all the wealth was owned by the *shoguns* and their *samurai*, their warriors. The rest of the population lived in cheap, paper-thin houses, inured to hunger and cold. In summers they simmered through the humid, sweltering heat; in winters they made tent-like wraps of rice straw, and wore straw snow boots. Because their houses were without heat, they wore heavily padded clothing to keep from perishing. Their food was principally rice, fish and tea, and not too much of that. But they learned to live with a flair, with a spiritual essence that lifted them above the mundane.

Their bit of fish was served on a plate or grass mat, made beautiful by a garnish of spring wild flowers or a sprig of autumn maple. They feasted the eye rather than the stomach. Every home was enriched by a "beauty corner," an alcove highlighted by an exquisitely simple flower arrangement. Above it hung a scroll, usually a short poem written in delicate calligraphy. In a Catholic European or Latin American home, the center of worship is a crucifix, a figure of the Virgin Mary, or a saint with a burning candle: in Japan their altar is the "beauty corner." They worship beauty. It lifts and heals their souls.

Not too much has changed. True, Japan has come into the 20th century with fierce eagerness. They have become modernized, mechanized, technicalized — and wealthy. But most of them still live with that same beautiful simplicity and quiet passion for loveliness that has characterized them for centuries.

Even their poetry epitomizes the chaste beauty of nature. Traditional poetry celebrates the change of seasons, often in some extremely subtle reference, although customarily openly expressed, as in this poem by Ryokan, written 150 years ago:

> *A long, misty day in spring:*
> *I saw it to a close, playing ball*
> *with the children.*
>
> *The breeze is fresh,*
> *the moon is clear.*
> *Together let us dance the night*
> *away, in what we have left of old age.*

Beauty Revives Youth

The Nobel Prize-winning Japanese author, Yasunari Kawabata, wrote in his slim volume, *Japan, The Beautiful, and Myself*:

"When we see the beauty of the snow, when we see the beauty of the cherries in bloom, when in short we brush against and are awakened by the beauty of the four seasons, it is then that we think most of those close to us, and want them to share the pleasure. The excitement of beauty calls forth strong fellow feelings, yearnings for companionship...The snow, the moon, the blossoms, words expressive of the seasons as they move one into another, include in the Japanese tradition the beauty of mountains and rivers and grasses and trees, of all the myriad manifestations of nature, of all human feelings as well." (Quoted by permission of Nobel Foundation.)

In the same book, Kawabata also tells us that Ryokan, at the age of 69, fell deeply in love with a young nun of 29. The beauty of youth is a stimulating restorative. Beauty, in all its forms, can be a magical potion for the heart, the flow of blood, the breathing, the digestion, the vigor of the body's muscles. Did you ever watch someone who has just fallen in love? No matter at what age, their eyes sparkle, their lips are full and red, their cheeks glowing. They are lively and eager for life. Beauty creates love, and love beauty.

Between the Tracks

Even in "gentile poverty," the not-so-affluent Japanese manage to create an aura of beauty. At the shabby little station near my home at the end of the "Toonerville Trolly Line" on the outskirts of Tokyo, they built a tiny pool between the tracks, surrounded by flowers and filled with darts of golden fish. In spring, the petals of cherry blossoms rolled across the platform, rosy wheels lifting my spirits into the sun. In the winter, snow sometimes piled deep on the old stone lantern. Even in the rush of one of the most modern, bustling, over-crowded, technocratic societies in the world, they still take time for beauty. Can that be why Japan has such an astonishingly low death rate from heart attacks and cancer?

Beauty Through All Your Senses

Taste it. Taste it in the first rich ripe strawberries of summer, with its sweet red succulence caressing your tongue with perfumed sunshine. Taste it in the tingling ping of rose champagne, sipped from a glass of crystal.

Smell beauty. Half the glory of taste comes through the nostrils. Those luscious berries, that fragrant champagne — the scent is as important as the taste. (Note: Older people lose much of their senses of taste and smell. Solution: 200 milligrams of zinc daily.)

Smell beauty in the wind from the sea, in the scent of sun-warmed pines in the mountains, in the rich aroma of new-turned earth in your garden, in the dizzying fragrance of June roses. Oh, I can think of so many beautiful smells.

Hear beauty. Turn off the TV and the electric mixer and the power lawn mower — and just listen to the beauty around you. Hear the mourning dove calling softly from the weeping willow in your neighbor's yard. Hear the robins singing their lovely bedtime song at sunset. Hear the squirrels chattering *pizzicato* in the big oak in the back yard. Hear the glass wind chimes playing a fragile song in the breeze off the bay. If you are really listening, each of those sounds will give you a shot of joy which will add zest to your day.

Sometimes we think of beauty as that which is visible only. But it is found by *all* our senses, even the sense of touch. Try stroking the satin finish of a carved wood quail, smoothed from ironwood into beauty by primitive Indians of Mexico. Feel it? Isn't it lovely?

Twice the Beauty

To share beauty with others is to enjoy twice the beauty. Look at Margaret Murdock, the tiny wisp of a woman who played the bells in the Campanile at the

University of California, Berkeley campus, until her retirement at the age of 87.

She had started as a bell ringer during the '20s, doing it simply for the joy of it, during her noon hour. Although she had a full-time job at the University, she took her lunch hour to send the music of the bells ringing out across the Bay. To look at the delicate white-haired little lady walking across the campus, one would never have dreamed she had the strength in her small hands to ring those bells. But sharing the beauty of "her" bells with the world was what kept her young. She lived to be 91, having given us "the beauty of the bells" for 60 wonderful years.

But you needn't be a bell ringer to share beauty with others. Maybe you can just cut a rose from your garden and take it to a friend. Or lend a friend a book of poetry from your library, containing something which thrilled you especially. Or make a table decoration for someone, using a little basket you chance to have, filling it with fresh, red-cheeked peaches from the store, and adorning the handle with a russet bow. Or make a flower arrangement from wild flowers and weeds you pick in an empty lot to share with someone. Double the beauty.

More beauty:

Japan, the Beautiful, and Myself, Yasunari Kawabata, Kodansha, Ltd., Tokyo, 1969. The Nobel Foundation sponsored the publication of this inspiring book, written by the best-selling Japanese novelist and Nobel prize winner, author of *Snow Country* and *Thousand Cranes*.

*Faith is the bird that sings
when the dawn is still dark.*
—Anonymous

21. LET NOTHING STOP YOU

When Cliff Wolfe developed throat cancer, and surgery removed his larynx, deprived him of his voice, ended his career as a New York architect and very nearly his life, he turned to writing poetry. This verse became his theme:

> **Songs**
> *There was a part of me
> that no longer sings
> I have lost my harp
> with all the sounding strings.
> An inner voice remembers
> old refrains,
> And I shall find a way
> to speak of inner things.*

It was his first poem, written at 73. Now 84, he has written more than a hundred poems, of which some 20 have been published and nine have won awards, including the Grand Prize at the Poetry Day banquet. And he has just been elected to the Board of the Ina Coolbrith Poetry Circle. He refused to let cancer conquer him.

Born Blind

I met a most remarkable young man recently, a young Russian Jew born in Kiev. His parents were both deaf, and when they met, fell in love at a school dance and were married, his father's mother was so terrified of them bringing another handicapped child into the world, she slept in their bedroom to keep them from consummating their marriage. Her attempt failed and the young couple had a fine healthy girl baby.

Five years later another child, Meir Schneider, was born, blind. During his early childhood, after the family escaped to Israel, he endured five torturing operations to restore his sight. They did little to help. He could only distinguish slightly between light and dark. He was declared legally blind and learned to read Braille.

And then he met a young teenager, younger than himself, who showed him how he could learn to control his own body in a process of self healing.

Today Meir Schneider, Ph.D., lives in San Francisco, and can read without glasses, living proof of his theories of the curative powers of the mind. He has won the use of his eyes through a lifetime of eye exercises and movement therapy. Through his practice, he has taught thousands of others the discovery of the body's own inner resources in curing disease, some diagnosed as "incurable."

His book, *Self Healing: My Life and Vision*, is an inspiration to all who read it. In it he tells of his long struggle to cure his blindness, a congenital disease.

Dr. Ray Gottlieb, O.D., Ph.D., says, "Meir's courage and imagination in developing a new therapy have been an inspiration for my own work for a decade."

Dr. Schneider is indeed an inspiring and innovative young man, who refused to allow being born blind become a permanent handicap.

If a Dancer Can't Dance...

..:What is left? Virginia Russ was a ballet dancer in San Francisco, a petite butterfly of a girl, pirouetting joyously across the stage and through life, shedding pleasure about her as an apple tree sheds petals. But that was many decades ago.

Her hips began giving her trouble. No more dancing.

She turned to writing. Exquisite poetry, and equally elegant prose. She began a novel, but it went slowly. The pain in her hips slowed her down. Finally, she had to have the hips replaced with artificial joints, and it was a long time before she was able to get back to the book. But she could walk again!

She was preparing to attend the convention of the National League of American Pen Women in Atlanta when she fell desperately ill. The doctor was unable to diagnose the problem, but it was clearly a life-and-death illness. It was finally found that she was having an allergic reaction to the material in the mechanical hips. They were hurriedly removed, leaving her without any joints in the hips.

But undaunted, Virginia resumed work on her novel. Slowly she recovered her health and joie de vivre. Knowing the remarkable artistry of her writing, her friends awaited impatiently for her book to get into print. The parts they had heard foretold a great book.

Through sheer grit and determination, Virginia learned to walk again, even without joints. Not only did she walk about the house, but she learned to hike about the wild country where she had retired. And once again she began going down to the lake every morning to swim in the icy water, rain or shine. For a woman of 80, her health was remarkable. Nothing could daunt Virginia.

Her novel was nearly finished. Then one morning, she smelled smoke. The house was afire. Scrambling into bedroom slippers and a bathrobe, she escaped — barely — with nothing but her life. The novel, and all those long years of writing, were gone up in smoke.

We didn't see Virginia for a long time. But we sent her gifts to help her through those terrible days. Then, to everyone's astonishment, she appeared in March at the Annual Poets Dinner in Berkeley! How was she? Oh, just fine, thank you! She was her usual sunny self, as animated and excited about life as ever. How was the novel coming? Oh, she was just too busy to get at it yet. Too busy writing poetry.

Nothing will ever get Virginia down. Her father lived to be 104. So will Virginia, no doubt.

Learn To Give Up?

It can be done, if you don't have the spunk and fire that Virginia and Meir and Cliff have. Scientists at Johns Hopkins University tried it with two rats. One they held firmly in the hand so that it could not escape, no matter how vigorously it struggled. Finally it gave up. Then they dropped it into a tank of warm water. It immediately sank, with no effort to swim, because it had learned to give up. Then they took a similar rat, which had not learned the bitter lesson of helplessness and hopelessness, and dropped it into the water. It immediately swam to safety. So, you see, "giving up" is a learned response.

"Whether you look at rats, dogs, or people," says Dr.

Martin E.P. Seligman of the University of Pennsylvania, who performed a similar experiment with dogs, "it's abundantly clear that those who try harder do better. Intelligent organisms automatically know how to help themselves: they keep trying; they have hope."

The healthy tendency does not have to be learned, says Seligman. But *helplessness must be taught*. We must never permit ourselves to learn it.

"We Do Not Grow Old...

...We become old by not growing," wrote 80-year-old Emma Selch in her Christmas letter. She is almost completely blind, a real tragedy for one who has always read voluminously and whose vocation is painting. But does she complain? Never.

Last year she was unable to attend the Silver Anniversary celebration of Colorado Mountain College to which she had been invited especially because she was the college's first librarian. We wanted to honor her. (See *Miracle on a Mountain* for the whole story.)

She sent her deep regrets. She was off on a tour of New Zealand.

You'll Never Walk Again

Nellie Duffy had just lost her husband, who would have been 82 in a few days. It was traumatic. She had been very young when they were married, and the prospect of living alone was appalling. But she was determined not to give in. She kept her job of writing news items for the local paper, as well as a historical column, *Pages of the Past*. She also helped with a book on the history of Glenwood Springs, Colorado.

When the house needed a bit of repair, she did it.

There was no Jim now to do it for her. One day, as she was up on a tall ladder behind the house, the ladder tipped. She fell on a heavy wood-adz, blade up in a pile of rocks. Her foot was almost completely severed.

"I'm going to have to remove the foot," the doctor told her. "It's broken in fourteen places, and the flesh is completely cut through. It's impossible to re-attach it."

"Sew it back on anyway!" was her answer.

"Very well," the doctor warned. "But you will have to suffer the results."

For three years Nellie hobbled around with a walker, but she was determined to walk again, normally. Finally, she discarded the walker and resumed her active stride — all over town, gathering items for the newspaper.

Valiant Warrior

When we taught in the same school in Tokyo, Kay Kawaguchi was a living dynamo. Young, bursting with originality and vitality, she touched the entire school through her music classes. She gave musicals, concerts, and programs of all sorts. Music was the heart of the school.

And then, one summer vacation, she suddenly went blind, totally and irreparably. And at the same time she was told that she was a victim of multiple sclerosis, that dread disease once known as "creeping paralysis," which slowly immobilizes the entire body. Not Kay! Not our beautiful, dynamic Kay! Oh, no!

Through the years I have kept track of her through friends, and have kept writing to her. Then I next heard that she was in the hospital with terminal cancer. Oh, dear God, no! She was hospitalized for two years. Finally she was dismissed, cured of cancer. Kay and that indomitable spirit!

One day I got a letter from her. Someone else had addressed it, but it had her name on the return. I opened it to find a brief note, scrawled awkwardly with a pencil. She had folded a thin sheet of paper in accordion folds, and feeling the creases with her finger tips had managed a childish note. What courage! Year by year she has continued writing, and now she writes with pen, neat, beautifully legible letters. They are always cheerful, telling about her latest hobby, never once mentioning her health or disability. Last year she was learning Braille, and this year she sent me the tape and manuscript of a lullaby she has written, in both Japanese and English.

The last time I visited her in Tokyo she opened the door of her apartment, as smilingly serene as ever. One would never have guessed her blindness.

"Can I make you some tea?" she asked, after we had settled in chairs.

"Oh no, thanks," I remonstrated. "Let's just sit and talk."

But ignoring my reply she went into the kitchen without hesitation and prepared our refreshments. Soon she returned, bearing a lovely tea tray with hot tea and cookies. I watched her in total dismay as she set the tray confidently on a low coffee table.

"Kay," I asked uncertainly, "can you see shapes? Or tell the difference between light and dark?" I couldn't believe that she was really blind, the way she moved easily and gracefully about the house.

"I see nothing but total blackness," she smiled, and then deftly switched the conversation to questions about mutual friends. The rest of our visit was light-hearted chatter. Kay has never learned to give up.

Others who refused to quit:

Reprieve, Agnes de Mill, G.K. Hall and Co., Boston, 1982.
    Heart-warming story of the famed dancer who refused
    to die. Highly recommended.
Miracle on a Mountain, Lucile Bogue, Strawberry Hill Press,
    San Francisco, 1987. The true story of building an
    international college from scratch on a Colorado
    mountainside, and of a dedicated community that
    refused to call it quits.
Self-Healing: My Life and Vision, Meir Schneider, Routledge
    and Kegan Paul, New York, 1987. The inspiring
    account of a young Russian Jewish refugee, born blind,
    who developed his own method of self-cure. Tells of
    the thousands he has helped.
Dare to Dream: the Rose Resnick Story, Rose Resnick,
    Strawberry Hill Press, San Francisco, 1988. Despite
    blindness from early childhood, the author has proven
    that one person can, indeed, change the world.
Her Story/Engagement Calendar, 1986. Planned Parenthood
    of Northwest New Jersey, Inc., 196 Speedwell Ave.,
    Morristown, NJ 07960. Contains biographies of over 50
    of America's most important women, the movers and
    shakers of their time. Nothing stopped them.
*Hopeful Living: How To Put Regeneration To Work In Your
    Life*, Bob Rodale, Rodale Press, Emmaus, PA, 1987
If You Could See What I Hear, Tom Sullivan, with Derek
    Gill, Harper and Row, New York, 1975. Autobiography
    of a young man, 28, born blind.
People in Peril and How They Survived, Reader's Digest
    Ass'n., 1983

*My heart goes where the wild goose goes
And I must go where the wild goose goes.
Wild goose, brother goose, which is best,
The wandering foot or the heart at rest?*
—Song of the 1950s

22. CULTIVATE ITCHY FEET

You're Never Too Old for Adventure

Lowell Thomas, the peripatetic reporter of far places, took himself a bride and a 70,000-mile honeymoon when he was 85. His first marriage had lasted 58 years until his wife's death. But widowhood didn't diminish his zest for travel, and so now for the honeymoon they went skiing in the Rockies of Canada, and visited the Dali Lama's 1000-room palace in Tibet.

Art Linkletter, a long-time friend, wired him at the Mandarin Hotel in Hong Kong: "LOWELL: I HAVE GREAT FAITH IN YOUR STRENGTH AND VIRILITY, BUT A HONEY-MOON LIKE THIS COULD BE FATAL." Thomas wired back: "IF SHE'S GOT TO GO, SHE'S GOT TO GO!"

He was just finishing another new book when he died at nearly 90.

The Traveling Tolles

They were born with passports in hand and "sand in their sandals." They met in the Austrian Alps where they were skiing, she selling encyclopedias door-to-door to pay her way, he on an after-college break. She had already taken a tramp-freighter jaunt to Tahiti. Two kindred souls, they were married immediately in Innsbruck and took a motorcycle honeymoon through

North Africa.

Undoubtedly, George and Marian are the most exciting traveling companions in the world. I have shared with them their blazing enthusiasms and eager curiosity in such far-flung places as Mexico, the Netherlands, Williamsburg (Virgina), Ecuador, San Francisco, and the Wilderness Area of the Colorado Rockies.

George Tolles is one of the most stable people I know, despite the lure of the open road. He has taught international relations and German (among other things) in the same college for 25 years, so it was time for a sabbatical. He took off to follow Marco Polo's tracks along the old "Silk Road," branching off wherever his curiosity took him. I had cards from him in Russia, China, Nepal. He was caught in an early snow in Tibet and was attacked by a pack of wild dogs in India.

Marian took a vacation to join him in Greece. I just received a card from them, picturing the mosques of Istanbul. Marian wrote: "Istanbul is an exotic mixture of East and West. We have seen splendid palaces, mosques & museums & spent hours exploring the Grand Bazaar & Egyptian Spice Market. But for me the highlight was a visit to the 300-year-old Hamam (Turkish baths) where I had the full treatment. Tomorrow by ferry through the Sea of Marmara to 'Canukkale—from there we visit Troy & Gallipoli. Love, Marian and George."

Another couple who will never grow old! Like fine wine, they only get better.

Be a Flexible Flyer

Travel is a case of mind over matter. If you're expecting the same kind of breakfast you have in your own kitchen back in Hoboken, forget it. If you get up angry because the lumpy bed is not your own Beautyrest mattress, you're wasting your travel money. If you're irritated by the crowds of other tourists who also want to be awed by Notre Dame Cathedral, too bad. If you're going to work yourself up into a first class tizzy when you have to stand in line with your luggage on the hot tarmac in Rome, you should have stayed home and shot your wad at MacDonald's, where things seldom change. If you're going to travel, relax and enjoy.

How Do We Start? And When? And Where?

If you haven't done much traveling up to this point, a good place to start is with your local university. For example, San Jose State University sponsors International Travel Study programs every summer. They advertise such spectacular tours as these:

MEXICO CITY: Summer Spanish Language Program;
ENGLAND: Palaces and Antiques;
CHINA AND TIBET;
KENYA ODYSSEY: Wildlife and Culture;
FALL FOLIAGE IN NEW ENGLAND;
HONG KONG: Bargain Shopping for the Holidays

Touring with a group does not appeal to some, but it is far easier for the beginner or the elderly, since the tour leader takes care of all the bothersome details. Even on tours, they give you plenty of free time to explore. They take care of your luggage, reservations, and local transportation, which can become a real hassle for the uninitiated.

All Aboard, Amtrack!

If you haven't seen all you want of these beautiful old United States, a good way to go is by Amtrack. They offer summer tour specials that are truly exhilarating — from the rugged coasts of Maine to the sandy beaches of San Diego, from the summer Theatre Festival in Seattle to Disneyworld and Key West in Florida. Plan to spend a week at least at your destination. There is always so much more beauty, culture, history and entertainment than you ever have time for. Amtrack is far less expensive that your own car, and leaves you free to enjoy the sights, rather than hassling with strange road maps, street signs, highways and parking.

Arrive Refreshed!

Before you go, call or write ahead to the local Visitors Bureau or Chamber of Commerce of the area you want to visit, asking them for everything available for visitors. They are usually quite generous with their glossy and exciting brochures, giving you the scoop on where to stay, where to eat, what to see, what to do. These are so enticing you can't wait for Amtrack to pull into the station.

Amtrack travel itself is a pleasure. It's not as plush as it was "in the good old days" when, as a little girl, I took a trip with Grandpa when he was running for U.S. Senator. No crisp white linen table cloths in the dining car, with waiters in elegant uniforms serving "Pheasant under glass with paté." But the food is good, and the child in me is still thrilled by the waiter running through the cars with his chimes, calling out "First call for dinner!"

It's fascinating to watch the map of America slipping past outside the windows, from the snow-capped Rockies to the purple sage of the deserts, from the white-steepled villages of New England to the red-tiled Spanish roofs of the Southwest.

My four-year-old grandson and I had a great adventure riding Amtrack from Oakland to Tucson for Christmas vacation one year. The train was loaded with dozens of other children on Christmas vacations, and they had a marvelous time, playing hide-and seek up and down the aisles. For me the high point of the trip was the glamorous old Spanish-style station in L.A., where we waited to changed to the Starlight Express, while I dreamed of the '20 and '30s, with all the Hollywood stars sweeping through these massive halls with their furs and diamonds and trailing entourages.

For Caddy it was the little roomette on the Starlight Express, where everything seemed to him to be built on a playhouse scale, from the tiny "bathroom" to the wee closet. He was charmed by having to climb a ladder to his upper bunk, a mattress swinging on a leather straps like a hammock.

Wagons Ho!

Or you can travel back in time as well. There are many innovative tours on the market if you keep your eyes open and read the travel pages. One that intrigues me is *Wagons Ho Wagon Train*, now based in Arizona, although it has been operating for many years in Kansas. It is a covered wagon tour across the desert near Phoenix (winters) and near the Grand Canyon (summers), staying out of sight of freeways and "civilization" on the four-day, three-night trek. The wagon train sports an old fashioned stage coach as well as the canvas-covered wagons.

The "pioneers," ranging in age from six to 84, dress in traditional blue jeans, cowboy hats, sunbonnets and long skirts. The trekkers enjoy the wide open spaces and the silences. No sounds but the rumbling of wagon wheels and the songs of turtle doves. They sleep under the stars and waken to the smell of mesquite smoke, and frying bacon, and fresh coffee bubbling over the campfire. During the day, they ride in the wagons, or hike along on foot, or ride horseback. Lunches and dinners are delivered by chuck wagon. Another concession to today's lifestyle: portable restrooms at each rest stop.

Ruth and Frank Hefner, who started this grand adventure 15 years ago, are flooded by letters from grateful guests. Wrote Mrs. R. Sheldon Jones, of Lafayette, "Many things touched me deeply and will for a long time, such as the trail where we saw the actual wagon-wheel ruts of those pioneers brave enough to journey to the unknown. My family and I wish we were back on Wagons Ho right now — *it hurt to leave!*"

Bon Voyage

An excellent way to satisfy your yearning to see and taste far ports and places is to take a cruise. There are as many price levels and destinations as there are potential "sailors" to take them. An easy way for the inexperienced traveler is to join AARP (the American Association of Retired Persons), although you need not be retired to join. You need only to be 50.

Next step, write to AARP Travel Service, giving them your AARP membership number, and ask them for information on cruises in the area you prefer. (They ask you to limit your request to three cruises.) This year they listed cruises to Alaska, Bermuda, the Caribbean, Europe, Hawaii, Mexican Riviera, Orient, South America, South Pacific, Transcanal, Transocean, and USA Waterways. Just listing these exciting choices makes me want to pack my bags and set out tomorrow.

Cruising is the lazy boy's way to go. And it's a wonderful way to travel if one of your family is incapacitated in any way. I had the joy of taking my invalid sister (confined to a wheelchair) on a week's cruise on the elegant Mississippi Queen (although I would have preferred the historical old Delta Queen, a floating palace; but it didn't have elevator service).

We "did" New Orleans for a couple of days before the cruise began, just to get the feel of the Deep South. On board we dined sumptuously and had a free floor show every night, along with plenty of Dixie Land jazz. They offered land tours at all the river towns where we tied up. I even had the rare treat of playing the steam calliope as we drew in to a river port. That trip was the highlight of dear Vernie's life.

It's an experience every red-blooded American shouldn't miss, a part of real American history come alive. I can still hear that calliope singing out across the wide Mississippi.

Cruisin' the Caribbees

The travel section of your local paper is full of enticing cruises. One of my more eventful adventures was a Caribbean cruise on the French liner, the M.S. Mermoz, one of the most exquisite ships afloat. With my 13-year-old granddaughter, we visited the Dominican Republic, St. Thomas in the Virgin Islands, Martinique, St. Croix, and Antigua.

Each island was an entirely different world in itself, different in scenery, cultural influences, national background, and languages — Danish, Spanish, French, English. Here is a marvelous way to begin savoring the fabulous differences of foreign lands without being "on your own," a plus for the beginning traveler. You're babied and coddled, not thrown into a foreign culture to sink or swim.

(Personally, I like the "sink or swim" approach, which I've enjoyed on four continents, but 13-year-old Becky hadn't. She was even afraid of the little Indonesian cabin boys on our ship, who were quite enamored of this beautiful blonde.)

If You'd Rather Walk

Modern Maturity had an exciting article in their February-March 1988 issue, entitled "America's Majestic Hikes," describing 10 top trails in national parks, a travel adventure much more to the taste of many of our vigorous, health-minded citizens than a leisurely high-calorie cruise.

In each of the parks are described a number of different trails, each so delightful one is tempted to set off at once, even with a wooden leg or a wheelchair. Send to AARP for this particular issue before it is out of print, or check it out at your local library.

They list the trails at Crater Lake in Oregon; Glacier National Park in Montana; Yellowstone Park in Wyoming; Isle Royal in Michigan; Great Smoky Mountains in Tennessee; Yosemite Park in California; Shenandoah Park in Virginia; Denali National Park in the heart of Alaska; Arches National Park in Utah; and Volcanoes National Park in Hawaii.

Fantastic! Utterly fantastic!

Holiday in Rent-Free Splendor

The best idea since the wheel is the trade-a-home plan. Several of my friends have spent their summer vacations in a foreign country, or even in some appealing spot in these United States, merely by trading homes through some reliable agency. Just listen:

"We spent three memorable weeks on an island-in-the-sun, living in a luxurious hilltop villa with a private swimming pool, private tennis court, air-conditioned car, and full-time housekeeper. The above items cost us nothing whatever, with the exception of the housekeeper, whose wages were $30 a week. In fact the plane tickets...were the only appreciable expense we incurred on our exotic vacation."

This sort of arrangement can be made through Vacation Exchange Club by filling out a detailed application form, then waiting until their catalog comes out with the listing of available homes and locales, and matching up with someone wanting to trade homes for a time compatable with you.

I know three different families who traded homes with families in England for the summer with great success, and I have already signed up with the Vacation

Exchange Club for next summer. I'll let you know how it turns out.

Some Travel Tips

1. Take along your sense of humor.
2. Relax. Don't get up-tight if things don't pan out.
3. Take along your childish sense of curiosity.
4. Read something beforehand about the country.
5. Take a dictionary of your host country.
6. Pack as few changes of clothing as you can manage.
7. Get information of climate, temperature and season, and pack accordingly.
8. Don't forget your passport.
9. Check on visa and immunization requirements. (Call US Government Passport Service nearest you. Allow plenty of time.)
10. Take plenty of money — in the form of traveler's checks — never much cash. Borrow some before you leave, if necessary to have a safe cushion. If you don't need it, you can repay it as soon as you get back.

Go Someplace!

Take a trip, if it's no more that to a B & B (bed and breakfast) in a nearby town. They can be lots of fun, too. I have found some to be quite an event. It will add zest — and years — to your life!

Your Best Friend

Go visit your travel agent. They don't cost you a cent, for their costs are born by the airlines, cruise ships, etc.

A good travel agent can be your best friend.
Bon Voyage!

Great travel ideas:

AARP Travel Service, P.O. Box 38997, Los Angeles, CA 90038.
National or worldwide travel, designed for over 50.

Above the Clouds Trekking, P.O. Box 398, Worcester, MA
01602. (800) 233-4499; in MA (617)799-4499.
Worldwide adventure for the discerning traveler. Exotic
mountain travel in unfamiliar, unknown territory.

All Aboard, Amtrack! For exciting travel ideas, call (800) USA-
RAIL and ask for unusual vacation information.

Colorado Trail, Regional Forester, U.S. Forest Service 11177
W. 8th Avenue, Box 25127, Lakewood, CO 80225.
Adventure for hikers in the Rockies.

Mississippi River Cruises, Delta Queen Steamboat Co., 511
Main Street, Cincinnati, OH 45202.

Paquet Cruises, Inc., 1370 Avenue of the Americas, New York
10019. For cruising the sunny isles of the Carribean in
the elegance of a French ocean liner. Super service.
French cuisine.

International Travel Study, Office of Continuing Education,
San Jose State University, San Jose, CA 95192-0135.

Travel Trips for Senior Citizens, U.S. Department of State
Publication 8970, Superintendent of Documents, U.S.
Government Printing Office, Washington, D.C. 20402.
A valuable little folder sponsored by the Bureau of
Consular Affairs, U.S. State Department. Essential for
anyone leaving the country for the first time, helpful
for even seasoned travelers.

Vacation Exchange Club, Inc. , 12006 111th Avenue, Unit
12, Youngtown, AZ 85363. Join for $25 membershp
fee, then exchange your home for your vacation with
anyone abroad who has a home to offer in the area of
your choice. Exciting possibilities.

Does he paint? he fain would write a poem—
Does he write? he fain would paint a picture.
—Robert Browning

23. THE FOUNTAIN OF YOUTH

Ponce De Leon discovered Florida in 1493, but he failed to find the mythical Fountain of Youth, for which he was searching. That's because there is no such thing as a magical potion. Youth is found in creating. The magic spring is within one's self. It restores — or sustains — youth by bringing forth beauty out of the inner depths of the mysterious unknown deep within us. There is something about the singing colors of paint that revive, restore, and set the heart to singing.

Luella Wolfe is a case in point. Confined to Hillhaven Convalescent Hospital in Oakland, she had the good fortune to be introduced to the magic of paints in her late 90s. For two hours a week she took an art class at the hospital. She could hardly wait for the next lesson. She soon began to accumulate quite a "portfolio," much admired by her peers and hospital staff. At 98, Luella Wolfe had her first "one-woman show." She began to sell some of her paintings. At 99, one of her paintings appeared on the front cover of Vista College catalog. By the time she was 102, one of her pieces was hanging in the governor's office of Sacramento.

"It makes me feel good and gives me a purpose, something to look forward to." Not a day passed without painting. As she was finishing up a commissioned water color, she remarked, "I was always crazy about art, but I didn't know I'd still be painting at over 100. And I never dreamed I'd be selling my work."

The Fountain of Age

Painters often demonstrate the rejuvenating influence of creating. Goya was stone deaf and very nearly blind. Both Monet and Cézanne continued to paint long after they were considered blind. Perhaps it is because they found their productive years slipping from them that they refused to waste a moment. They continued to paint madly, using every waking hour to continue bringing up to the surface all that beauty and genius that was still lying deep within them. They knew it was there and couldn't bear to quit while part of it was yet uncovered. Their productive years were unbelievable.

Titian, who lived to be 100 at a time when life expectancy was about 35, perhaps would have lived even longer had he not been caught by a plague that was sweeping Europe. An art critic of the time reports visiting him in his studio when he was past 90 and finding him "brush in hand, painting."

The Years Rest Kindly on Artists

Whatever the magic is, it is indeed potent. Grandma Moses is so famous in this respect that her story hardly needs repeating. Anna Mary Moses, 76, gave in to the misery of arthritis and neuritis, giving up embroidering because she could no longer hold the needle. It occurred to her she might try a bit of painting, for she loved gay colors. She had never tried it, but she thought she might manage to hold a paint brush.

The results are history, with galleries and private collections around the world brightened by her colorful primitives of New England scenes. The year after her 100th birthday, Grandma Moses made 25 paintings. She lived to be 101, a worldwide legend.

The Miracle of Paint

In 1890 a 15-year-old boy living in Santa Clara submitted a handful of cartoons to W.R. Hearst at the San Francisco *Examiner*. To his delight, they were accepted, with a request for more, becoming the first comic strip in America. Young Jim Swinnerton became more popular daily. But at 28, he faced tragedy. He was diagnosed as suffering from terminal tuberculosis, with a year to live.

He fled to the desert to die alone, taking along his ink and sketch pad. He couldn't let Hearst down as long as he was able to hold a pen.

As a final adventure, he went to Arizona Territory to visit Indian country and the wondrous canyons he had vaguely heard mentioned. He was so intoxicated by its beauty, he rushed back to the nearest town to order oil paints and a huge roll of canvas. He had to record some of this unbelievable color while he was still living — these gorgeous reds and purples and turquoise skies and vermillion cliffs.

Swinnerton continued to paint until he was 97.

The Magic Fountain

But it isn't just paint. This same magic is found in all the arts. Creating seems to produce some magic chemical inside our own bodies that gushes forth like Ponce De Leon's mythic spring, triggered by the mere act of creating something beautiful and original. And by its entering our veins, it strengthens our immune system which fights disease and spurs the production of endorphins. This literally makes us younger in body.

It Could Be Music

Aaron Copland, beloved American composer, should be in the autumn of life, but he still exhibits all the lilt and joy of his *Appalachian Spring*. His 85th birthday was celebrated four years ago by an all-Copland retrospective televised by PBS.

"It's one of the most interesting programs of my work imaginable!" he said. "It makes getting to be 85 a delight!"

Fountain of Words

Writing is yet another art that carries a compelling eternal youthfulness in its creation. As I sit at my typewriter day after day, I forget time, place, age, health. I am not myself. I am an eager instrument of some irresistible force outside myself which flows through my mind and fingers, recording its message on the page. For me, writing is not a hobby which I do in my spare time. It is a compulsion. It is life.

I am sure other writers would say the same thing. It isn't something you choose to "do" or "not do." Once that fiery liquid, creativity, has been loosed in your veins, there is no resisting it. Sometimes the first intoxicating experience does not come until late in life, but when it grips you, there is no turning back.

George Bernard Shaw is one of the best known of long-lived authors, having written his last Broadway show, *Buoyant Billions*, at 93. It starred Colleen Dewhurst and Jason Robard, their first co-starring vehicle, 1949. Noted for his rapier wit and hilarious humor, he continued poking holes in human frailties until he dicd at 94. His plays are still favorites with theatre-goers around the world.

The Point Is...

...You can do it, too. Although you may never become another Grandma Moses or George Bernard Shaw, the wonderful world of creativity is open to everyone. The arts are something you do because you love doing them.

See if you can locate an adult art class somewhere. Or go to your library and find a book on painting, or sketching, or modeling clay figures. Go to a hobby shop and find something that catches your eye. Or to an art supply store and find pastel crayons in a luscious array of colors.

Take a class in *ikebana* or flower arranging. All you need is a handful of weeds, a bowl and a bit of instruction. Haruko Obata came to San Francisco when she was ten, and soon began a lifelong study of flower arranging. Today, at 97, she is still sharing that joy with others, still giving classes in the art of *ikebana.*

Write your autobiography. This can be stimulating, as well as creating a valuable record of the past to be left to your descendents. Don't worry about your writing skills. The main thing is to get it down. Open up. Lay your life out in the light of day for the first time. Art Isitt, 84, has just published his!

If you're serious about staying young, *create* something!

Guideposts to the Fountain of Youth:

The Crown of Life: Artistic Creativity in Old Age, Hugo
Munsterberg, Harcourt Brace Jovanovich, New York,
1983. An exploration of the excellence achieved by
famous painters, sculptors, architects, and other artists
in advanced age.

Help for the autobiographer:

Tracing Your Roots, by the editors of Consumers Guide, Bell
Publishing Co., New York, 1977
Beginner's Ancestor Research Kit, Philip Breck, Bristol
Publishing Enterprises, San Leandro, CA, 1990
How You Can Trace Your Family Roots, Ron Playle, R and D
Services, P.O. Box 644, Des Moines, IA

Fear death? —to feel the fog in my throat,
The mist in my face.
—Robert Browning

24. FACE YOUR FEARS

When Sharon was a toddler, she loved playing a game with her father which she called, "Catch me." She wanted him to chase her, and off she would race, as fast as her little legs would go, squealing in hysterical "terror" as she went, half in play, half in earnest. But just before he overtook her, her real terror would win out and she would whirl to face him, not able to continue the cat-and-mouse game.

Today's world is a hotbed of terrors — very real fears, not a child's make-believe "scare me" game. Nuclear wars, terrorism, violence in the streets and invading the sanctity of our homes, drug wars, AIDS, our disappearing ozone protection, toxic wastes, terrifying weather changes, man-made desertification of the earth, increasing cancer rate...

I won't go on. It's too depressing. And besides, this book is written to raise your spirits, not depress them.

We have faced life frankly in previous chapters, and this will be no exception. Let's face our fears with courage. If you are willing to look your fears in the eye, you will conquer them like Sharon did when she faced the "bogy man."

Life is a Pattern

It all fits together somehow, in some grand pre-conceived pattern which we cannot clearly see. We are too close to it. Just as we cannot see "the boot" of Italy from either land or sea; it is only from 30,000 feet up that the "boot" is revealed.

Life is birth, growth, adolescence, maturity, procreation, aging and death, in that order. That's life. Yet is that all there is to it? By no means! It is love, joy, beauty, creation, laughter, work and play, sharing and preserving this glorious earth. And oh, so much more! But the exquisite basic pattern often baffles us by its complexity.

Looking back on your own life and that of your family, you will no doubt find great pleasure and countless happy memories connected with the first five steps of this pattern — birth, growth, adolescence, maturity, and procreation. It is only when you come to Number 6 and 7, aging and death, you want to look the other way. But that's what this book is all about — aging — healthily and happily.

So we've made it this far. Now let's face the last and natural steps — final illness and death. Don't be afraid to talk about it. That's the only way to drive your fears away — by honestly facing them.

Some people are squeamish. They say, "Don't talk about such things. It's too depressing. Let's think of something pleasant."

Fine. If you want to be an ostrich. But I prefer to be an intelligent human, to look ahead, to weigh the options to problems that may arise, and then face the remainder of my life in calm serenity. I want the last part of my mysterious pattern to be as rich and fulfilling as the rest. I do not fear death. When the time comes, I'll be ready.

What Do *You* Fear?

Natalie Gulbrandsen, former President of Unitarian Universalist Women's Federation, says that the greatest fears of growing old are disease, nursing homes, mental and physical senility and death.

Maggi Kuhn, founder of the Gray Panthers, lists the greatest fears as widowhood, menopause, retirement, and death of friends.

My personal list is: nursing homes, with the helplessness and uncaring neglect often found there; loss of independence; unbearable pain and blindness.

Let's look at fears, one at a time. How can I conquer them?

The Show Must Go On

Incontinence is a prevalent health problem that most of us are embarrassed to face. Those afflicted used to stay home, close to the bathroom, and plead illness — or disinterest — anything to avoid the humiliation of having a public accident. Either that or go to church smelling like an unchanged baby, or worse still, like a sleazy public toilet. All this happens oftener than we care to admit.

But now, like rape, it has come out into the open and can be treated with honesty.

I had surgery for it, which did nothing to help. As excited about "living fully" as I am, I couldn't see myself resigned to a life of housebound invalidism. But I was terrified of leaving home, even for a trip to the supermarket.

And then they invented *Depends*. And later *Attends*. And I had suddenly regained my youth and freedom!

Thanks, June Allyson, for your buoyant TV commercials. Thank you, thank you, thank you! My life is again back on "full steam ahead."

Disease

Disease I can take, if and when it comes. I have experienced so many, one more seems to instill no awe in me. If I get one, I'll either recover — or I won't. Or I'll research it until I know my options. Of course I'm doing everything possible to avoid disease, as the previous chapters indicate, but I'm not losing any sleep over the subject.

Cancer, I believe, is dormant in practically everyone at my age. But I plan to allow it to lie there inactive, or at least developing slowly, as it does in older people, if one is otherwise strong and healthy and in top physical condition. *If* the growth is not spurred into activity by emotional or physical trauma. Even a biopsy can be a trauma to the body. I prefer to allow myself to die naturally, rather than to traumatize my body with surgery, chemotherapy or radiation. I am healthy, happy and productive right now.

And I could never again fully recover from the trauma of surgery, aside from the valuable time I would lose from my productive life. Let's not rock the boat. I've reached a nice ripe age.

Hope for Cancer Patients

Carl Simonton, MD, with his wife Stephanie, operates the world-famous Cancer Counseling and Research Center in Dallas. They have achieved phenomenal success with their program, teaching patients to use relaxation and mental imagery as an integral part of the

Center's treatment program.

Love, Medicine and Miracles

Bernie Siegel, MD, had added the magic potion of "love" to the Simonton cancer treatment. Let me quote from the back of Dr. Siegel's book:

"Miracles are happening to exceptional patients every day — patients who have the courage to work with their doctors to participate in and influence their own recovery. *Love, Medicine and Miracles* shows you how."

The hopeful attitude he instills in the reader is a good dose of medicine in itself. But the information he gives, along with the exciting case histories of "remissions" or cures, gives one real hope.

Senility

If I'm mentally senile, I won't care anyway. It may be hard on my family, but I will eventually become unaware. I just hope others will be patient, knowing they may be in my shoes some day.

If I'm physically senile, I'll regret not being able to hike up and down the California hills, or maybe not even up and down stairs to the bathroom. But I am enrolled in a Home Care insurance plan which should allow me to have someone in to give me the help I need. Home Care is much less expensive than a nursing home and far more pleasant.

Widowhood and Dragons

I must admit fresh widowhood almost destroyed me. I seriously considered suicide. As my husband lay dying for many long weeks (lung cancer, surgery and complications), I told myself I could take it with my head up. That was before he died — Christmas week. We had been married on Christmas Day, 41 years earlier.

I wrote poetry to release my pain, which has always been my way of coping.

Help for the Widowed

Locally it's called Widow's Network Center, although the title may vary in other areas. It's a support group for new widows and widowers, with a group counseling center. There are people there who have been through it themselves, and can be of great assistance and comfort.

Another support group is sponsored by the American Association of Retired Persons. If you are newly bereaved, do get in touch with them.

Just hang in there and remember: *time is the greatest comforter.*

Menopause is a Piece of Cake

To tell you the truth, I didn't even know when my menopause occurred. I only know that some time in my 50s, it dawned on me that this momentous occasion had come and gone without my being aware of it.

I was so engrossed in the founding of a college during those years (see *Miracle on a Mountain*), I forgot myself.

Here is the secret of surviving: 1. Don't worry about it. 2. Keep fully occupied. Some women think of menopause as the end of their youth—the beginning of old age. Nonsense! In some women it occurs in their

30s, in others not until their 40s or 50s. Mine occurred in my 50s, but that certainly didn't make me an old lady. I was still as young and vital as I'd ever been. And it had no effect on my sex life.

Men Too?

Yes, some men, too, fear this "mid-life crisis" or male menopause. Medical science now tells us that there are some indications of a possible physical change in men at mid-life, but so minor as to be negligible. The male mid-life crisis is mostly psychological, the fear of losing the sex drive, of becoming impotent. Balderdash! The world is full of men who have fathered children at 70, 80 and 90. Sex is ageless.

You can make love at any age. And you can dream about it, even if you don't do it. I know one gentleman, 94, who enjoys reading his *Playboy Magazine* in his room in the nursing home.

Olivia Whiteman, a charming and attractive lady of 97 who spent her last years in a rest home, was pestered by an ardent admirer, another resident. She had her family bring her a water pistol, which she kept filled and near at hand. This weapon proved quite effective in cooling her lover's ardor, she reported.

Death of Friends

This is a real fear, especially of the loss of dear friends who are suffering from serious illness. My own response to this is to pour my love and care and prayers into their recovery. I show them my constant love and thought in many ways — telephone calls, visits, get-well cards, love notes, and little gifts. And four of my most beloved friends have recovered during the past two years from possible terminal illnesses.

If my devotion had no effect on their recovery, at least it eased their suffering a little to know that they were so loved. Love works miracles, as Siegel says.

He tells us that infants who do not receive love will waste away and die, even under the best conditions of sanitation and nutrition. He also tells of an experiment done by Harvard psychologists, showing that merely watching a film of Mother Theresa and her work of love "increases the levels of immunoglobulin-A in the saliva, the first line of defense against colds and other viral diseases." Love is a very real medicine. Use it.

Retirement Homes

Many people solve this problem by choosing to sell their own homes and move into a retirement home while they are still strong and able. The wise ones check first to see if the home provides nursing home or hospital care when one becomes incapacitated. And by "check" I mean talk with people who have really had experience in the home. Don't rely merely on vague promises made in the sales office.

One beautiful retirement community I know promises hospital care when residents become helpless, but a resident who had lost her husband there told me the hospital care was a joke. I have a friend in another retirement community who has been in and out of the hospital several times during the past year, and receives excellent attention. Make inquiries.

Don't Be an Ostrich

It's easy to push the thought of loss of independence into dark shadows and ignore the possibilities which we may one day have to face. Easier now — but far harder in the future. Again I prefer to face my future head-on, while I am healthy, happy, full of living, and able to make wise choices without pressure.

I have visited nursing homes in my area. I have visited friends who are patients. I have found some homes I would not put a cat in, yet where I visited a beloved friend week after week. It breaks one's heart. Most of her friends refused to go with me.

"I can't stand it," they would say. "It's too depressing."

It was depressing. Yet she had to live in it, not just visit. Her family put her there because it was something they could afford.

How to Measure a Nursing Home

Smell. The first thing I look for is a fresh clean smell — or better still, no smell at all. If you detect the odor of stale urine, watch out! You know then that the patients are neglected. Also beware of the heavy scent of fresh deodorant, sprayed just before visiting hours.

Visit during nonvisiting hours. You certainly won't be welcome, but enter quietly and purposefully, without asking any questions, and walk briskly through the halls as though you were there on a special errand.

Sounds. Listen for laughter, a good sign. But if you hear prolonged screams — a red light. It may be only a demented patient, not someone being tortured. But it can be devastating for patients forced to listen to it. Or the pound of loud rock music, to which many insensitive staff seem to be addicted. It can be used to mask real calls for assistance (sometimes deliberately).

Prolonged and repeated calls of "Nurse! Nurse! I

need the toilet!" are another warning. Or the rude or angry voice of any staff member. These you will discover only during nonvisiting hours, for they usually put their best foot forward when they expect visitors.

Appearance. It is not my first priority, but it is a guide to the quality of the place. Is it bright and airy and colorful? Are there lovely pictures on the wall? Is there a beautiful flower arrangement somewhere? Are the floors quiet and carpeted? Are the staff members pleasant, happy-looking people? Is the exterior attractive? Is it someplace you would want to have your friends visit?

Dining room. Facilities are of utmost importance, as well as the food served. Arrange to share a meal (either by formal reservation or by subterfuge, if necessary) with the patients. It can range from "great" to "garbage." I know. I've tried both.

Activities are important too. Look for the weekly or monthly calendar. They have one posted, if they have activities of which they are proud.

Faces of the patients are a pretty good barometer. If they smile at you when you enter, you're in the right place. But if the residents sit in their wheelchairs like zombies, half-asleep, you can be pretty sure that they have been sedated to keep them quiet. Or if they glare back at you angrily, you may count on an unfriendly or even hostile environment.

Chaparral House

I have found the place I want to go if the need arises. It's Chaparral House at the end of a quiet street in Berkeley. It has everything I want in a home, fulfilling all the guidelines I have mentioned.

A low rambling building surrounded by gardens, trees and flowers, it has an aura of charm and graciousness from the moment you walk into the wide, open lobby. I was greeted by a beautiful young woman, Rev. Johanna Boeke, a Unitarian minister.

Although Chaparral House is nonprofit and nondenominational, it provides a chaplain for personal counseling, as well as to give discussion groups and Sunday morning worship service. "Jopie" is warm, friendly and loving. You know, as she shows you through the place, introducing you to the smiling, happy residents. You meet people in wheel chairs, some who are walking, all of them attractively dressed, with their hair nicely done. (A beauty shop down the hall explains the fresh hair-dos.)

You meet Mary Jean Froehlich, the Activities Director, a spirited young lady who keeps things humming. The calendar is brimming with activities from daily exercises to Saturday painting classes, from Monday singalongs to Wednesday happy hours, from bridge to coffee klatches, from discussion groups to concerts in Golden Gate Park. It's a happy place, and the faces of the people I met proved it, from staff to residents.

One charming resident I met has the distinction of being Berkeley's oldest resident. Her eyes are bright and alert, laughter ready to bubble up a any moment. Her niece, Elizabeth Lodge Rees, M.D., says she is "funny, uncomplaining, and a joy to be around." Charlotte Orr Howard will be 110 next August 4. "It's been a great life," she laughs. "But I'll be ready to go up to join Frank any day."

Another healthy sign of the livability is the lively newsletter *Chaparral Chatter*, published for members on a monthly basis. It is brimming with birthdays, inspirational columns, "Garden Gossip" (giving the latest scoop on the House's backyard garden), and a fine column by Rev. Boeke.

See why I would choose Chaparral?

Blindness

Here is another bugaboo that haunts me — because I live by my eyes. My writing, my research, my very extensive correspondence around the world, my constant reading in a variety of fields. Everything I do depends upon my eyes, which have never been very good and are definitely not getting any better.

But if you'll remember my young friend Kay Kawaguchi, who went blind one summer vacation, you remember that she has let nothing stop her.

I may even continue to write my books. If Kay can learn to put her music on tape, I can surely learn to dictate my books on tape.

Reading is one occupation I would dread giving up. My house is bursting with books. I read constantly.

But even this fear I have faced — Books For the Blind, out of the Library of Congress. In fact, three of my own books are available to the blind. I have already found that most, if not all the states, have a State Library for the Blind, which can be called on an 800 number.

Terminal Pain

To face this fear, one we all share, I'm sure, I was introduced to the solution by my beloved friend, Portia

Mansfield, who lived a most exuberant and utterly delightful 92 years. When still in her "young" 80s, she began working enthusiastically for the euthanasia movement in America, believing that "death with dignity" was everyone's right. I too joined the "death with dignity" movement, worldwide. I belong to the Hemlock Society, a magnificent organization in this field. (Hemlock Society, P.O. Box 11830, Eugene, OR 97440-3900).

Freedom of Choice

When life begins, a baby's birth is a cause for great joy and celebration. When we have lived a full and wonderful life, we should also celebrate the end — with something akin to a harvest celebration. It should be the happy culmination to a rich life.

But too often the end is marred by prolonged illness and unthinkable suffering. We have become conditioned to fear and death. We deserve better. A life worth living should be worth dying for — with dignity. The end of life is inevitable. Why not face it as our last great adventure? Let it be an adventure — into the unknown!

The ethical complexities are enormous in seeking ways to ease and accelerate the inevitable end. Yet the state of California is seeking to do just that. Knowing that legislators face intense pressure from both "for" and "against" constituents, the people themselves have petitioned to have a ballot initiative in the fall election for The Humane and Dignified Death Act, bringing it straight to the voters. (Late note: Insufficient signers were registered in time for the current election, but we will try again.)

With the enormous surge of suffering and death from the world-wide AIDS epidemic, it is time we faced our mortality courageously.

A Man of Vision and Courage

As Governor Lamm of Colorado wrote in his fine book, *Megatraumas*:

"Modern medicine and technology have made death degrading, painful, prolonged, and even profane. We prefer a quick and painless death to a slow, painful one.

"We seek 'one more pill' to allow us compassionate control over our own bodies. A slow death is not only degrading but has forced millions into bankruptcy and/or poverty. We don't force life upon our terminally ill dogs and other pets; yet...society refuses dying people release.

"...We are making daily sacrifices of prolonged suffering to the new secular god, technology.

"Zeno...stated more than two thousand years ago: 'The wise man will...make his own exit from life...if he suffers intolerable pain, mutilation, or incurable disease.' After all these years, we as a society are not even to the point where Zeno started. We should have an absolute right to effect our own ends."

The Light at the End of the Tunnel

Last April I attended the seventh Biennial Conference of the World Federation of Right-to-Die Societies, hosted by the Hemlock Society.

We listened to speakers from Canada, the Netherlands, England, France, the United States — a variety of accents and experiences, but all the same basic thought: Let's bring dignity to death. Let's allow doctors to cease, legally, prolonging life past the desire of the terminally ill patient.

As Rev. Boeke wrote in one of her columns in *Chaparral Chatter*:

"I believe that life is a gift, and we have a responsibility to treat that life with respect and reverence, living the best we can and with as much dignity and kindness as possible, meeting each new challenge with openness and courage."

Life Without Fear

Refuse to worry. It gets you nowhere. Face your fears honestly. If there is anything you can do about them — do it! If not, put them aside and forget them, for worry does nothing but intensify them.

Death is just one more milestone in life's bold adventure, so let's be ready for it. The final curtain will end a great show!

Help with your fears:

Common Sense Suicide: The Final Right, Doris Portwood, Hemlock/Grove, New York, 1983

Compassionate Crimes, Broken Taboos, Edited by Derek Humphrey, Hemlock Society, 1986

Deciding to Forego Life-Sustaining Treatment, by the President's Commission for the Study of Ethical Problems in Medicine and biomedical Research, Published by Concern for Dying, Suite 831, New York, NY 10107. Ethical, medical, and legal issues in treatment decisions.

Euthanasia and Religion, Gerald A. Larue, Hemlock Society, 1985. A survey of the attitudes of world religions to the right-to-die. Dr. Larue is Emeritus Professor of Biblical History and Archeology at the School of

Religion, U of S. California, Los Angeles.

Getting Well Again, O. Carl Simonton, M.D. and Stephanie Matthews-Simonton, Bantam, New York, 1981. The Simontons' revolutionary life-saving self-awareness techniques used in cancer treatment in their Fort Worth Cancer counseling Center.

Humane and Dignified Death, Robert L. Risley, Americans Against Human Suffering, Glendale, CA 1987. A new law permitted physician aid-in-dying. Introduction by Derek Humphrey.

Knowing Your Rights, edited by AARP, 1985. Another good reason for joining American Association of Retired Persons, 1909 K St. NW, Washington, DC 20049.

Jean's Way: A Love Story, Derek Humphrey and Ann Wickett. Hemlock, Grove, New York, 1978. A loving young Englishman assists his terminally ill wife. "...a powerful plea for voluntary euthanasia — the individual's right to death in peace and dignity." -Arthur Koestler

Megatraumas, Richard D. Lamm. Houghton Mifflin Co., New York, 1985. Governor Lamm's thoughtful and compassionate book on death made degrading, painful, prolonged, and even profane by modern medicine and technology. He seeks a way to gain control over our own bodies.

Nursing Homes: How to Evaluate and Select a Nursing Home, People's Medical Society, Emmaus, PA, 1983.

On Death and Dying, Elisabeth Kubler-Ross, Macmillan, New York, 1969.

The Parkinson Patient at Home, Robert S. Schwab, MD and Lewis J. Doshay, MD, Parkinson's Disease Foundation, New York, 1981. For the patient who is not responding well to levodopa therapy.

To Call It a Day—In Good Season, Newell Brown, Joyous Publications, P.O. Box 9002 #375, Boulder, CO 80303, 1986. How not to overstay one's life. Out of print; mimeographed copies $5.

Whose Life Is It Anyway?, Brian Clark, Dodd, Mead and Co.,
    New York, 1978. A play from England, touching and
    funny, takes an uplifting view of death. Overwhelming
    tribute to life.
The Woman Said Yes, Jessamyn West, Harcourt Brace
    Jovanovich, New York, 1976. The account, honestly
    told, of America's beloved author, Jessamyn West,
    assisting her dying sister, Carmen, in a voluntary death.
    Deeply moving and upbeat story, courageously revealed.

Organizations to help you face your fears:

Alzheimer's Disease and Related Disorders Association,
    800-621-0379 (in Illinois 800-572-5037). Call for a
    support group near you.
Alzheimer's Disease Research, 15825 Shady Grove Road,
    Suite 140, Rockville, MD 20850, (301) 948-3244.
    Publishes *Alzheimer's Research Review*
American Association of Homes for the Aging, 1129 20th St.
    NW, Suite 400, Washington, DC 20036. Free packet of
    brochures if you send a stamped (2 first class stamps)
    self-addressed legal size envelope.
Americans Against Human Suffering, P.O. Box 11001,
    Glendale, CA 91206-7001, (818) 240-1986. Political
    action arm of the Hemlock Society, advocating Death
    With Dignity.
AARP, 1909 K. St. NW, Washington, DC 20049. Send a
    postcard to request these free publications: *Miles Away
    and Still Caring* (D12748) for long distance care-givers;
    Handbook About Care in the Home (D955) describes
    home health-care services nationwide; *The Right Place
    at the Right Time* (D12381) gives types of long term
    care services available; *Coping and Caring: Living with
    Alzheimer's Disease* (D12441) for families of patients.
Books for the Blind, Library of Congress, 1291 Taylor St.
    NW, Washington, DC 20542. (202) 287-5100. Or call
    your State Library for the Blind for books on tape.
Cancer Counseling and Research Center, O. Carl Simonton,
    MD, Director, 6060 N. Central Expwy. Suite 140, Dallas,

TX 75206. (214) 373-7744. Write for information on their remarkably successful program teaching patients relaxation and imagery techniques.

Children of Aging Parents, 2761 Trenton Rd., Levittown, PA 19056. Offers help from your local support group.

Concern for Dying, Donald W. McKinney, President, 250 W. 57th St., New York, NY 10107. Educational council for the Living Will. Publishes excellent newsletter for any voluntary contribution.

Hemlock Society, Derek Humphrey, Executive Director, P.O. Box 11830, Eugene, OR 97440-3900, (503) 342-5748. Supports the option of active voluntary euthanasia for the terminally ill.

Humane Sciences Press, Inc., 72 5th Avenue, New York, NY 10011-8004. Publishes a catalog of publications on Aging, Death, Dying and Religion.

National Association of Home Care, 519 C Street NE, Stanton Park, Washington, DC 20002. Information regarding home-care agencies.

National Ass'n. of Area Agencies on Aging, 600 Maryland Avenue SW, Suite 208, Washington, DC 20024. Local Area Agencies on Aging give free advice on adult day care, respite care, home health aid, transportation and escort services, homemaker and chore services, housing services and support groups. Look in phone book for Area Agencies on Aging; if unavailable, write to above address.

The National Council on the Aging, Inc., NCOA Publications, PO Box 7227 Ben Franklin Station, Washington, DC 20044. Write for their list of helpful publications.

National Cancer Institute, Office of Cancer Communications, Bldg. 31, Bethesda, MD 20014. Call 800-638-6694. Excellent info on counseling, treatment, financial aid, medical facilities, educational materials, list of Cancer Centers.

National Office: Make Today Count, PO Box 303, Burlington, IA 52601. Monthly newsletter $10/yr. Self-help for cancer patients, families and professionals.

National Office: American Cancer Society, 777 3rd Avenue, New York, NY 10017. Advice on practical aspects, rehabilitation and coping problems.

National Rehabilitation Information Center, 800-34-NARIC or (202) 635-5826. Call 9 AM to 5 PM, EST, Monday through Friday. Info on needs of people with physical limitations.

Parkinson's Disease Foundation, Wm. Black Medical Research Bldg., Columbia University Medical Center, 640-450 W. 168th St., New York, NY 10032.

The Suicide Education Institute of Boston, 437 Newtonville Avenue, Newton, MA 02150. (617)332-5165.

Widowed Persons Service, 1909 K St., Washington, DC 20049. (202)728-4370. Support group for the newly bereaved, or those who find it pending.

Further excellent sources of help in these books:

The Age Center Sourcebook, Jean Crichton, Simon and Schuster. Covers financial, medical and emotional problems of the aging.

Home Health Care Solution, Janet Zhun Nassif, Harper and Row. Consumer-care guide, shortcuts, tax-saving advice.

Who Cares? Andrus Volunteers, Andrus Gerontology Center, USC, University Park/MC 0191, Los Angeles, CA 90089-0191. $7.50 postpaid, +.42 sales tax for California residents.

Resource and reading list for living with cancer, available from Lifeline Institute, 5501 Fair Oaks St., Pittsburgh, PA 15217 (412) 521-2290

And a Time to Live—Toward Emotional Well-Being During the Crisis of Cancer, Robert C. Cantor, Harper and Row, $3.95

Whoever Said Life is Fair—Growing through Life's Injustices, Sara Kay Cohen, Charles Scribner and Sons, New York, $7.95

Cancer Care—Where To Go, Whom To See, What Will Happen, Harold Glucksburg, M.D. and Jack D. Singer,

Johns Hopkins Press, $14.95. Excellent! Most comprehensive book available.

Mind Over Cancer (cassette tape), Lynn Gray, $9.50 ppd. or $10 for tape with following book:

Living With Cancer—How To Help Your Doctors Help You Back To Health, $3

The Courage To Live—Techniques To Cope With Stress, Depression, Crisis, Plans for Living to the Fullest, Bantam Books, 1979 $2.75

Why Me? What Every Woman Should Know About Breast Cancer To Save Her Life, Rose Kushnes, Signet books, 1977 $2.50

You Can Fight for Your Life—Emotional Factors in the Causation of Cancer, Lawrence Le Shan, 1977.

Realistic Alternatives in Cancer Treatment, Marion Morra and Eve Potts, Avon Press, 1980 $8.98

Mind as Healer, Mind as Slayer, Kenneth Peltier, Dell Publishing, 1977

Good Grief—A Constructive Approach to the Problem of Loss, Granger E. Westberg, Fortress Press, $.150

Health care catalogs:

Dr. Leonard's Health Care Catalog, 74 20th St., Brooklyn, NY 11232

Walter Drake's Health Care Catalog, 388 Drake Bldg., Colorado Springs, CO 80940

Help with incontinence:

To Life!, Kimberly-Clark, Dept. KC-390, 2100 Winchester Road, Neenah, WI 54956. Inspiring magazine, designed for those who have the handicap.

Help for Incontinent People, P.O. Box 544PE, KC-390, Union, SC 29379. HIP is a non-profit group assisting and informing health professionals and the public.

The Simon Foundation, P.O. Box 835 KC-390, Wilmette, IL 60091. Publishes a quarterly newsletter, The Informer, and offers a hardbound book, Managing Incontinence: A Guide to Living with the Loss of Bladder Control. Send self-addressed envelope

Do your joys with age diminish?
When mine fail me I'll complain.
Must in death your daylight finish?
My sun sets to rise again.
—Robert Browning

25. IT'S UP TO YOU

Secrets

"What is your secret?" people have been asking me for years. "How do you get so much done? How do you have so much energy? How can you stay so young?"

What is the answer? I began to analyze myself, my life, my beliefs. To answer some of these questions for myself, I have set down a few guideposts.

These "secrets" really came first, the skeleton of the book, before I did ten years of research and came up with *How to Stay Young Forever.* Here they are, for what they're worth.

1. Have something exciting to look forward to each morning. Have a goal for every day.
2. Love living! Don't just pass through life.
3. Keep a healthy mind. Don't hold grudges. Accentuate the positive.
4. Keep an active mind. Think! And read, read, read! Unplug the TV.
5. Make life a window, not a mirror. Be interested in others. Don't join the "me" generation.
6. Don't pity yourself. Forget yourself.
7. Accept new challenges. Don't be afraid to try something new.

8. Keep busy. I love hiking, travel, museums, art galleries, gardening, opera, ballet, history. Whatever appeals to you.
9. Be physically active. I walk two brisk miles daily, carrying my groceries up a steep hill and up the stairs.
10. Get plenty of rest. I need more sleep and rest now than I ever did. Eight to ten hours a night, plus one or two daytime naps make me feel wonderful.
11. Get plenty of love. Keep in touch with family and friends often, by visits, phone calls or notes. Have several "best" friends, to avoid the "end of the world" when you lose one, as you inevitably will.
12. Avoid doctors whenever possible. But get a flu shot every fall! And keep track of that blood pressure! Keep it down by exercise and right living if you would avoid stroke.
13. Avoid drugs.
14. Avoid tobacco.
15. Avoid alcohol.
16. Drink eight glasses of water daily.
17. Avoid coffee, tea, caffeine.
18. Eat to stay healthy.
    a. Eat fresh fruit and vegetables daily.
    b. Eat whole grains and nuts. Avoid white flour.
    c. Eat fish, chicken, and turkey, removing fat and skin.
    d. Eat beef rarely.
    e. Avoid all processed foods whenever possible.
    f. Avoid sugar, salt, and fats.

g. Avoid pork, ham, bacon, and lunch meats.

It Takes a Long Time To Become Young (Pablo Picasso)

Bonnie gave me a birthday card with that legend on the cover. Inside it said, "Happy Birthday — Happy every day!" And below she had written, "And thanks for helping me to grow younger, too!"

I'm placing the odds on beating my genes. My mother died of cancer at 64, my father died of a heart attack at 82. My grandparents died at relatively young ages, but I plan to break a family record of longevity. The way I feel now, I'll make 100 easy. Maybe longer.

Grow Old Along With Me—the Best People Are Doing It!

The goal set for this book is not necessarily to lengthen your life, but to make it richer, fuller, more inspiring. It's the quality of life that is of value, not necessarily the length. But in looking back over the lives I have recounted, the richer and more interesting lives are also the longest.

Your life is yours, to do with as you see fit. It's not too late. It can be a great adventure.

Aging with grace:

The Challenge of Age: A Guide to Growing Older in Health and Happiness, Fritz Schmerl, M.D. with Sally Patterson Tubach, Continuum, NY, 1986. Living guide for aging with grace, by an 87-year-old genontologist.

Stay Young and Live Longer, Paul G. Neimark and Jay H. Schmidt, Budlong Press Co., Chicago, 1977. A doctor discusses how to stay young, and why you should want to. A priceless little book.